Heaven

compiled from the writings of

ELLEN G. WHITE

Pacific Press® Publishing Association
Nampa, Idaho
Oshawa, Ontario, Canada
www.pacificpress.com

Cover design by Willie Duke
Cover illustration by Lee Christiansen
Inside design by Steve Lanto

Library of Congress Cataloging-in-Publication Data
White, Ellen Gould Harmon, 1827-1915.
Heaven / Ellen G. White
p. cm.
ISBN 13: 978-0-8163-1981-7
ISBN 10: 0-8163-1981-2
1. Heaven—Christianity. 2. Seventh-day Adventists—Doctrines. I. Title.
BT846.3.W48 2003
236'.24—dc21   2002193126

08 09 10 11 12 • 6 5 4 3

Abbreviations
of Sources

ML   *My Life Today*
MM   *Medical Ministry*
1MR   *Manuscript Releases,* vol. 1
       (2MR, etc., for vols. 2-19)
Ms   Manuscript
OHC   *Our High Calling*
PCP   *Peter's Counsel to Parents*
PK   *Prophets and Kings*
PP   *Patriarchs and Prophets*
RH   *Review and Herald*
1SAT   *Sermons and Talks,* vol. 1
       (2SAT for vol. 2)
SC   *Steps to Christ*
1SG   *Spiritual Gifts,* vol. 1
       (2SG, etc., for vols. 2-4)
1SM   *Selected Messages,* book 1
       (2SG, etc., for books 2 and 3)
SD   *Sons and Daughters of God*
1SP   *Spirit of Prophecy,* vol. 1
       (2SP, etc., for vols. 2-4)
SR   *The Story of Redemption*
ST   *The Signs of the Times*
1T   *Testimonies for the Church*, vol. 1
       (2T, etc., for vols. 2-9)
TDG   *This Day With God*
TM   *Testimonies to Ministers and Gospel Workers*
TMK   *That I May Know Him*
UL   *The Upward Look*
YI   *The Youth's Instructor*
1888   *The Ellen G. White 1888 Materials*

Preface

Throughout the centuries the promise of Jesus in John 14:2, 3 has filled the hearts of Christians with hope: "In my Father's house are many mansions: if it were not so, I would have told you. I go to prepare a place for you. And if I go and prepare a place for you, I will come again, and receive you unto myself, that where I am, there ye may be also." In the darkest moments of despair, disappointment, despondency, or defeat, the hope of living with Jesus in heaven has brightened the day, cleared away the clouds, and lifted the spirits.

Heaven. What will it be like? Words are inadequate to describe it, but the Holy Scriptures give us glimpses of the glorious future. There all will be harmony, peace, love, and unity. All will be purity, holiness, and blessedness. Gone will be sorrow, crying, and pain. Best of all, death will be no more.

"There we shall know even as also we are known. There the loves and sympathies that God has planted in the soul will find truest and sweetest exercise. The pure communion with holy beings, the harmonious social life with the blessed angels and with the faithful ones of all ages, the sacred fellowship that binds together 'the whole family in heaven and earth'—all are among the experiences of the hereafter."—*Education,* p. 306.

We look forward with joyous anticipation to the day when Jesus will return to earth, not as a Man of sorrows but as King of kings and Lord of lords. In that day the dead in Christ will rise first, then His followers who are alive will be "changed, in a moment, in the twinkling of an eye" (1 Cor. 15:51, 52), and together this redeemed company, now immortal, will travel through time and space to the Paradise of God, to heaven itself.

This book provides glorious pictures of the future life both in heaven and on the New Earth. It enables one to hear by faith the thrilling music sung by angels and the redeemed. It excites one with the prospect of engaging in fascinating occupations and enterprises. As you sense the wonder and reality of the future life, may you determine to be among the citizens of heaven, and live forever in that land "where we never grow old."

BOARD OF TRUSTEES OF THE
ELLEN G. WHITE ESTATE.

Contents

Let us consider most earnestly the blessed hereafter. Let our faith pierce through every cloud of darkness and behold Him who died for the sins of the world. He has opened the gates of paradise to all who receive and believe on Him. To them He gives power to become the sons and daughters of God. Let the afflictions which pain us so grievously become instructive lessons, teaching us to press forward toward the mark of the prize of our high calling in Christ. Let us be encouraged by the thought that the Lord is soon to come. Let this hope gladden our hearts. . . .

We are homeward bound. He who loved us so much as to die for us hath builded for us a city. The New Jerusalem is our place of rest. There will be no sadness in the city of God. No wail of sorrow, no dirge of crushed hopes and buried affections, will ever more be heard. Soon the garments of heaviness will be changed for the wedding garment. Soon we shall witness the coronation of our King. Those whose lives have been hidden with Christ, those who on this earth have fought the good fight of faith, will shine forth with the Redeemer's glory in the kingdom of God.—9T 286, 287.

1

The Way to Heaven

BY JESUS ALONE.—"Let not your heart be troubled," He [Jesus] said; "ye believe in God, believe also in Me. In My Father's house are many mansions: if it were not so, I would have told you. I go to prepare a place for you. And if I go and prepare a place for you, I will come again, and receive you unto Myself; that where I am, there ye may be also. And whither I go ye know, and the way ye know." For your sake I came into the world. I am working in your behalf. When I go away, I shall still work earnestly for you. I came into the world to reveal Myself to you, that you might believe. I go to the Father to cooperate with Him in your behalf.

The object of Christ's departure was the opposite of what the disciples feared. It did not mean a final separation. He was going to prepare a place for them, that He might come again, and receive them unto Himself. While

He was building mansions for them, they were to build characters after the divine similitude.

Still the disciples were perplexed. Thomas, always troubled by doubts, said, "Lord, we know not whither Thou goest; and how can we know the way? Jesus saith unto him, I am the way, the truth, and the life; no man cometh unto the Father, but by Me. If ye had known Me, ye should have known My Father also: and from henceforth ye know Him, and have seen Him."

There are not many ways to heaven. Each one may not choose his own way. Christ says, "I am the way: . . . no man cometh unto the Father, but by Me." Since the first gospel sermon was preached, when in Eden it was declared that the seed of the woman should bruise the serpent's head, Christ had been uplifted as the way, the truth, and the life. He was the way when Adam lived, when Abel presented to God the blood of the slain lamb, representing the blood of the Redeemer. Christ was the way by which patriarchs and prophets were saved. He is the way by which alone we can have access to God.—DA 663.

THE SURETY OF OUR DELIVERANCE.—By His humanity, Christ touched humanity; by His divinity, He lays hold upon the throne of God. As the Son of man, He gave us an example of obedience; as the Son of God, He gives us power to obey. It was Christ who from the bush on Mount Horeb spoke to Moses saying, "I AM THAT I AM. . . . Thus shalt thou say unto the children of Israel, I AM hath sent me unto you." Exodus 3:14. This was the pledge of Israel's deliverance. So when He came "in the likeness of men," He declared Himself the I AM. The Child of Bethlehem, the meek and lowly Saviour, is God "manifest in the flesh." 1 Timothy 3:16. And to us He says: "I AM the Good Shepherd." "I AM the living Bread." "I AM the Way, the Truth, and the Life." "All power is given unto Me in heaven and in earth." John 10:11; 6:51; 14:6; Matthew 28:18. I AM the assurance of every promise. I AM; be not afraid. "God with us" is the surety of our deliverance from sin, the assurance of our power to obey the law of heaven.—DA 24, 25.

HELP OTHERS FIND JESUS, THE WAY.—Christ gave Himself to a shameful, agonizing death, showing His great travail of soul to save the perishing. Oh, Christ is able, Christ is willing, Christ is longing, to save all who will come unto Him! Talk to souls in peril and get them to behold Jesus upon the cross, dying to make it possible for Him to pardon. Talk to the sinner with your own heart overflowing with the tender, pitying love of Christ. Let there be deep earnestness; but not a harsh, loud note should be heard from the one who is trying to win the soul to look and live. First have your own soul consecrated to God. As you look upon our Intercessor in heaven, let your heart be broken. Then, softened and subdued, you can address repenting sinners as one who realizes the power of redeeming love.

Pray with these souls, by faith bringing them to the foot of the cross; carry their minds up with your mind, and fix the eye of faith where you look, upon Jesus the Sin Bearer. Get them to look away from their poor, sinful selves to the Saviour, and the victory is won. They behold for themselves the Lamb of God that taketh away the sin of the world. They see the Way, the Truth, the Life. The Sun of Righteousness sheds its bright beams into the heart. The strong tide of redeeming love pours into the parched and thirsty soul, and the sinner is saved to Jesus Christ.

Christ crucified—talk it, pray it, sing it, and it will break and win hearts. This is the power and wisdom of God to gather souls for Christ. Formal, set phrases, the presentation of merely argumentative subjects, is productive of little good. The melting love of God in the hearts of the workers will be recognized by those for whom they labor. Souls are thirsting for the waters of life. Do not be empty cisterns. If you reveal the love of Christ to them, you may lead the hungering, thirsting ones to Jesus, and He will give them the bread of life and the water of salvation.—6T 66, 67.

THE TRUE PATH THAT LEADS TO HEAVEN.—Many are losing the right way, in consequence of thinking that they must climb to heaven, that they must do something to merit the favor of God. They seek to make themselves better by their own unaided efforts. This they can never accomplish. Christ has made the way by dying our Sacrifice, by living our Example, by becoming our great High Priest. He declares, "I am the way, the truth, and the life." If by any effort of our own we could advance one step toward the ladder, the words of Christ would not be true. But when we accept Christ, good works will appear as fruitful evidence that we are in the way of life, that Christ is our way, and that we are treading the true path that leads to heaven. —RH November 4, 1890.

2

His Promise Will Be Fulfilled

KEYNOTE OF SCRIPTURES.—One of the most solemn and yet most glorious truths revealed in the Bible is that of Christ's second coming to complete the great work of redemption. To God's pilgrim people, so long left to sojourn in "the region and shadow of death," a precious, joy-inspiring hope is given in the promise of His appearing, who is "the resurrection and the life," to "bring home again His banished." The doctrine of the second advent is the very keynote of the Sacred Scriptures. From the day when the first pair turned their sorrowing steps from Eden, the children of faith have waited the coming of the Promised One to break the destroyer's power and bring them again to the lost Paradise.

Holy men of old looked forward to the advent of the Messiah in glory, as the consummation of their hope. Enoch, only the seventh in descent from them that dwelt in Eden, he who for three centuries on earth walked with his God, was permitted to behold from afar the coming of the Deliverer. "Behold," he declared, "the Lord cometh with ten thousands of His saints, to execute judgment upon all." Jude 14, 15. The patriarch Job in the night of his affliction exclaimed with unshaken trust: "I know that my Redeemer liveth, and that He shall stand at the latter day upon the earth: . . . in my flesh shall I see God: whom I shall see for myself, and mine eyes shall behold, and not another." Job 19:25-27.—GC 299.

To Take His People Home.—Christ has declared that He will come the second time to gather His faithful ones to Himself: "Then shall all the tribes of the earth mourn, and they shall see the Son of man coming in the clouds of heaven with power and great glory. And He shall send His angels with a great sound of a trumpet, and they shall gather together His elect from the four winds, from one end of heaven to the other." Matthew 24:30, 31.—GC 37.

The promise of Christ's second coming was ever to be kept fresh in the minds of His disciples. The same Jesus whom they had seen ascending into heaven, would come again, to take to Himself those who here below give themselves to His service. The same voice that had said to them, "Lo, I am with you alway, even unto the end," would bid them welcome to His presence in the heavenly kingdom.—AA 33.

The proclamation of Christ's coming should now be, as when made by the angels to the shepherds of Bethlehem, good tidings of great joy. Those who really love the Saviour cannot but hail with gladness the announcement founded upon the Word of God that He in whom their hopes of eternal life are centered is coming again, not to be insulted, despised, and rejected, as at His first advent, but in power and glory, to redeem His people. It is those who do not love the Saviour that desire Him to remain away, and there can be no more conclusive evidence that the churches have departed from God than the irritation and animosity excited by this Heaven-sent message.—GC 339, 340.

These truths, as presented in Revelation 14 in connection with "the everlasting gospel," will distinguish the church of Christ at the time of His appearing. For as the result of the threefold message it is announced: "Here are they that keep the commandments of God, and the faith of Jesus." And this message is the last to be given before the coming of the Lord. Immediately following its proclamation the Son of man is seen by the prophet, coming in glory to reap the harvest of the earth.—GC 453, 454.

Freedom From Sin.—This earth has been trodden by the Son of God. He came to bring men light and life, to set them free from the bondage of sin. He is coming again in power and great glory, to receive to Himself those who during this life have followed in His footsteps.—Letter 117, 1903 quoted in MM 20, 21.

"The Redemption of the Purchased Possession."— God's original purpose in the creation of the earth is fulfilled as it is made the eternal abode of the redeemed. "The righteous shall inherit the land, and dwell therein for ever." The time has come to which holy men have looked with longing since the flaming sword barred the first pair from Eden—the time for "the redemption of the purchased possession." The earth originally given to man as his kingdom, betrayed by him into the hands of Satan, and so long held by the mighty foe, has been brought back by the great plan of redemption.

All that was lost by the first Adam will be restored by the second. The prophet says, "O Tower of the flock, the strong hold of the daughter of Zion, unto Thee shall it come, even the first dominion." And Paul points forward to the "redemption of the purchased possession."

God created the earth to be the abode of holy, happy beings. That purpose will be fulfilled when, renewed by the power of God and freed from sin and sorrow, it shall become the eternal home of the redeemed.—RH October 22, 1908 quoted in AH 540.

To Make All Things New.—The work of redemption will be complete. In the place where sin abounded, God's grace much more abounds. The earth itself, the very field that Satan claims as his, is to be not only ransomed but exalted. Our little world, under the curse of sin the one dark blot in His glorious creation, will be honored above all other worlds in the universe of God. Here, where the Son of God tabernacled in humanity; where the King of glory lived and suffered and died—here, when He shall make all things new, the tabernacle of God shall be with men, "and He will dwell with them, and they shall be His people, and God Himself shall be with them, and be their

God." And through endless ages as the redeemed walk in the light of the Lord, they will praise Him for His unspeakable Gift—Immanuel, "God with us."—DA 26.

COST OF REDEMPTION REALIZED.—Never can the cost of our redemption be realized until the redeemed shall stand with the Redeemer before the throne of God. Then as the glories of the eternal home burst upon our enraptured senses we shall remember that Jesus left all this for us, that He not only became an exile from the heavenly courts, but for us took the risk of failure and eternal loss. Then we shall cast our crowns at His feet, and raise the song, "Worthy is the Lamb that was slain to receive power, and riches, and wisdom, and strength, and honor, and glory, and blessing." Revelation 5:12.—DA 131.

EARTH'S PURPOSE FULFILLED.—God created the earth to be the abode of holy, happy beings. The Lord "formed the earth and made it; He hath established it, He created it not in vain, He formed it to be inhabited." Isaiah 45:18. That purpose will be fulfilled, when, renewed by the power of God, and freed from sin and sorrow, it shall become the eternal abode of the redeemed. "The righteous shall inherit the land, and dwell therein forever." "And there shall be no more curse: but the throne of God and of the Lamb shall be in it; and His servants shall serve Him." Psalm 37:29; Revelation 22:3.—PP 67.

JESUS SUFFERED TO SAVE.—I saw the beauty of heaven. I heard the angels sing their rapturous songs, ascribing praise, honor, and glory to Jesus. I could then realize something of the wondrous love of the Son of God. He left all the glory, all the honor which He had in heaven, and was so interested for our salvation that He patiently and meekly bore every indignity and slight which man could heap upon Him. He was wounded, smitten, and bruised; He was stretched on Calvary's cross and suffered the most agonizing death to save us from death, that we might be washed in His blood and be raised up to live with Him in the mansions He is preparing for us, to enjoy the light and glory of heaven, to hear the angels sing, and to sing with them.—1T 123, 124.

3

The Second Coming Promised Throughout History

KEY TO HISTORY.—An understanding of the hope of Christ's second coming is the key that unlocks all the history that follows, and explains all the future lessons.—Letter 218, 1906 quoted in Ev 220.

TOLD TO ENOCH.—"And Enoch also, the seventh from Adam, prophesied of these, saying, Behold, the Lord cometh with ten thousands of his saints" (Jude 14). . . . The doctrine of Christ's coming was made known at this early date to the man who walked with God in continual communion. The godly character of this prophet is to represent the state of holiness to which the people of God must attain who expect to be translated to heaven.—RH July 31, 1888 quoted in TMK 348.

SACRIFICES A PERPETUAL REMINDER.—In patriarchal times the sacrificial offerings connected with divine worship constituted a perpetual reminder of the coming of a Saviour, and thus it was with the entire ritual of the sanctuary services throughout Israel's history. In the ministration of the tabernacle, and of the temple that afterward took its place, the people were taught each day, by means of types and shadows, the great truths relative to the advent of Christ as Redeemer, Priest, and King; and once each year their minds were carried forward to the closing events of the great controversy between Christ and Satan, the final purification of the universe from sin and sinners.

The sacrifices and offerings of the Mosaic ritual were ever pointing toward a better service, even a heavenly. The earthly sanctuary was "a figure for the time then present," in which were offered both gifts and sacrifices; its two holy places were "patterns of things in the heavens;" for Christ, our great High Priest, is today "a minister of the sanctuary, and of the true tabernacle, which the Lord pitched, and not man." Hebrews 9:9, 23; 8:2.—PK 684, 685.

The slaying of the Passover lamb was a shadow of the death of Christ. Says Paul: "Christ our Passover is sacrificed for us." 1 Corinthians 5:7. The sheaf of first fruits, which at the time of the Passover was waved before the Lord, was typical of the resurrection of Christ. Paul says, in speaking of the resurrection of the Lord and of all His people: "Christ the first fruits; afterward they that are Christ's at His coming." 1 Corinthians 15:23. Like the wave sheaf, which was the first ripe grain gathered before the harvest, Christ is the first fruits of that immortal harvest of redeemed ones that at the future resurrection shall be gathered into the garner of God.—GC 399.

GOOD NEWS.—The gospel message proclaimed by Christ's disciples was the announcement of His first advent to the world. It bore to men the good tidings of salvation through faith in Him. It pointed forward to His second coming in glory to redeem His people, and it set before men the hope, through faith and obedience, of sharing the inheritance of the saints in light. This message is given to men today, and at this time there is coupled with it the announcement of Christ's second coming as at hand. The signs which He Himself gave of His coming have been fulfilled, and by the teaching of God's Word we may know that the Lord is at the door.

John in the Revelation foretells the proclamation of the gospel message just before Christ's second coming. He beholds an angel flying "in the midst of heaven, having the everlasting gospel to preach unto them that dwell on the earth, and to every nation, and kindred, and tongue, and people, saying with a loud voice, Fear God, and give glory to Him; for the hour of His judgment is come." Revelation 14:6, 7.

In the prophecy this warning of the judgment, with its connected messages, is followed by the coming of the Son of man in the clouds of heaven. The proclamation of the judgment is an announcement of Christ's second coming as at hand. And this proclamation is called the everlasting gospel. Thus the preaching of Christ's second coming, the announcement of its nearness, is shown to be an essential part of the gospel message.—COL 226-228.

THE PRAYER JESUS TAUGHT.—*"Thy kingdom come."* *Matthew 6:10.*

God is our Father, who loves and cares for us as His children; He is also the great King of the universe. The interests of His kingdom are our interests, and we are to work for its upbuilding.

The disciples of Christ were looking for the immediate coming of the kingdom of His glory, but in giving them this prayer Jesus taught that the kingdom was not then to be established. They were to pray for its coming as an event yet future. But this petition was also an assurance to them. While they were not to behold the coming of the kingdom in their day, the fact that Jesus bade them pray for it is evidence that in God's own time it will surely come.

The kingdom of God's grace is now being established, as day by day hearts that have been full of sin and rebellion yield to the sovereignty of His love. But the full establishment of the kingdom of His glory will not take place until the second coming of Christ to this world. "The kingdom and dominion, and the greatness of the kingdom under the whole heaven," is to be given to "the people of the saints of the Most High." Daniel 7:27. They shall inherit the kingdom prepared for them "from the foundation of the world." Matthew 25:34. And Christ will take to Himself His great power and will reign.

The heavenly gates are again to be lifted up, and with ten thousand times ten thousand and thousands of thousands of holy ones, our Saviour will come forth as King of kings and Lord of lords. Jehovah Immanuel "shall be king over all the earth: in that day shall there be one Lord, and His name one." "The tabernacle of God" shall be with men, "and He will dwell with them, and they shall be His people, and God Himself shall be with them, and be their God." Zechariah 14:9; Revelation 21:3.

But before that coming, Jesus said, "This gospel of the kingdom shall be preached in all the world for a witness unto all nations." Matthew 24:14. His kingdom will not come until the good tidings of His grace have been carried to all the earth. Hence, as we give ourselves to God, and win other souls to Him, we hasten the coming of His kingdom. Only those who devote themselves to His service, saying, "Here am I; send me" (Isaiah 6:8), to open blind eyes, to turn men "from darkness to light and from the power of Satan unto God, that they may receive forgiveness of sins and inheritance among them which are sanctified" (Acts 26:18)—they alone pray in sincerity, "Thy kingdom come."—MB 107-109.

PROMISE GAVE JOY.—As Christ ascended, His hands outstretched to bless His disciples, a cloud of angels received Him and hid Him from their sight. As the disciples looked with straining eyes for the last glimpse of their ascending Lord, two angels from the rejoicing throng stood by them and said, "Ye men of Galilee, why stand ye gazing up into heaven? this same Jesus, which is taken up from you into heaven, shall so come in like manner as ye have seen him go into heaven" (Acts 1:11).

The disciples were filled with great joy. Over and over again they repeated the words Christ had spoken to them in His last lessons, as recorded in the fourteenth, fifteenth, sixteenth, and seventeenth chapters of John; and every one had something to say about the instruction, especially with regard to the words of the fourteenth of John . . .

The promise that He would come again, and also the thought that He had left them His peace, filled their hearts with joy.—Letter 55, 1886 quoted in UL 357.

JOHN SAW HISTORY OF GOD'S PEOPLE.—John was strengthened to live in the presence of his glorified Lord. Then before his wondering vision were opened the glories of heaven. He was permitted to see the throne of God and, looking beyond the conflicts of earth, to behold the white-robed throng of the redeemed. He heard the music of the heavenly angels and the triumphant songs of those who had overcome by the blood of the Lamb and the word of their testimony. In the revelation given to him there was unfolded scene after scene of thrilling interest in the experience of the people of God, and the history of the church foretold to the very close of time. In figures and symbols, subjects of vast importance were presented to John, which he was to record, that the people of God living in his age and in future ages might have an intelligent understanding of the perils and conflicts before them.—AA 582, 583.

PROPHECY REASSURES.—We must have a knowledge of the Scriptures, that we may trace down the lines of prophecy and . . . see that the day is approaching, so that with increased zeal and effort we may exhort one another to faithfulness. . . . Give up our faith? lose our confidence? become impatient? No, no. We will not think of such a thing. . . . See how the specifications of the prophecies have been and are fulfilling. Let us lift up our heads and rejoice, for our redemption draweth nigh. It is nearer than when we first believed. Shall we not wait patiently, filled with courage and faith? Shall we not make ready a people to stand in the day of final reckoning?—RH July 31, 1888 quoted in TMK 348.

HIS PROMISE GIVES COURAGE.—More than eighteen hundred years have passed since the Saviour gave the promise of His coming. Throughout the centuries His words have filled with courage the hearts of His faithful ones. The promise has not yet been fulfilled . . . but none the less sure is the word that has been spoken.—RH November 13, 1913 quoted in OHC 367.

4

God's People Delivered

GOD MANIFESTS HIS POWER AT MIDNIGHT.—By the people of God a voice, clear and melodious, is heard, saying, "Look up," and lifting their eyes to the heavens, they behold the bow of promise. The black, angry clouds that covered the firmament are parted, and like Stephen they look up steadfastly into heaven and see the glory of God and the Son of man seated upon His throne. In His divine form they discern the marks of His humiliation; and from His lips they hear the request presented before His Father and the holy angels: "I will that they also, whom Thou hast given Me, be with Me where I am." John 17:24.

Again a voice, musical and triumphant, is heard, saying: "They come! they come! holy, harmless, and undefiled. They have kept the word of My patience; they shall walk among the angels;" and the pale, quivering lips of those who have held fast their faith utter a shout of victory.

It is at midnight that God manifests His power for the deliverance of His people. The sun appears, shining in its strength. Signs and wonders follow in quick succession. The wicked look with terror and amazement upon the scene, while the righteous behold with solemn joy the tokens of their deliverance. Everything in nature seems turned out of its course. The streams cease to flow. Dark, heavy clouds come up and clash against each other. In the midst of the angry heavens is one clear space of indescribable glory, whence comes the voice of God like the sound of many waters, saying: "It is done." Revelation 16:17.—GC 636.

THE FOUNDATIONS OF THE EARTH SEEM TO BE GIVING WAY.—There is a mighty earthquake. The firmament appears to open and shut. The glory from the throne of God seems flashing through. The mountains shake like a reed in the wind, and ragged rocks are scattered on every side. There is a roar as of a coming tempest. The sea is lashed into fury. There is heard the shriek of the hurricane, like the voice of demons upon a mission of destruction. The whole earth heaves and swells like the waves of the sea. Its surface is breaking up. Its very foundations seem to be giving way. Mountain chains are sinking. Inhabited islands disappear with their living freight. The seaports that have become like Sodom for wickedness are swallowed up by the angry waters. Great hailstones, every one "about the weight of a talent," [Revelation 16:21] are doing their work of destruction. The proudest cities of the earth are laid low. The costly palaces, upon which

the world's great men have lavished their wealth in order
to glorify themselves, are crumbling to ruin before their
eyes.—4SP 453, 454.

A SPECIAL RESURRECTION BEFORE JESUS APPEARS.—
Graves are opened, and "many of them that sleep in the
dust of the earth . . . awake, some to everlasting life, and
some to shame and everlasting contempt." Daniel 12:2.
All who have died in the faith of the third angel's message
come forth from the tomb glorified, to hear God's covenant of peace with those who have kept His law. "They
also which pierced Him" (Revelation 1:7), those that
mocked and derided Christ's dying agonies, and the most
violent opposers of His truth and His people, are raised to
behold Him in His glory and to see the honor placed upon
the loyal and obedient.

Thick clouds still cover the sky; yet the sun now and
then breaks through, appearing like the avenging eye of Jehovah. Fierce lightnings leap from the heavens, enveloping
the earth in a sheet of flame. Above the terrific roar of thunder, voices, mysterious and awful, declare the doom of the
wicked. The words spoken are not comprehended by all;
but they are distinctly understood by the false teachers. Those
who a little before were so reckless, so boastful and defiant,
so exultant in their cruelty to God's commandment-
keeping people, are now overwhelmed with consternation
and shuddering in fear. Their wails are heard above the sound
of the elements. Demons acknowledge the deity of Christ
and tremble before His power, while men are supplicating
for mercy and groveling in abject terror.—GC 637, 638.

THE TEN COMMANDMENTS REVEALED TO ALL IN THE SKY.—Through a rift in the clouds, there beams a star whose brilliancy is increased fourfold in contrast with the darkness. It speaks hope and joy to the faithful, but severity and wrath to the transgressors of God's law. Those who have sacrificed all for Christ are now secure, hidden as in the secret of the Lord's pavilion. They have been tested, and before the world and the despisers of truth they have evinced their fidelity to Him who died for them.

A marvelous change has come over those who have held fast their integrity in the very face of death. They have been suddenly delivered from the dark and terrible tyranny of men transformed to demons. Their faces, so lately pale, anxious, and haggard, are now aglow with wonder, faith, and love. Their voices rise in triumphant song: "God is our refuge and strength, a very present help in trouble. Therefore will not we fear, though the earth be removed, and though the mountains be carried into the midst of the sea; though the waters thereof roar and be troubled, though the mountains shake with the swelling thereof." [Psalm 46:1-3].

While these words of holy trust ascend to God, the clouds sweep back, and the starry heavens are seen, unspeakably glorious in contrast with the black and angry firmament on either side. The glory of heaven is beaming from the gates ajar. Then there appears against the sky a hand holding two tables of stone folded together. The hand opens the tables, and there are revealed the precepts of the decalogue, traced as with a pen of fire. The words are so plain that all can read them. Memory is aroused, the darkness of superstition and heresy is swept from every mind, and God's ten words, brief, comprehensive, and authoritative, are presented to the view of all the inhabitants of earth. Wonderful code! wonderful occasion!—4SP 456, 457.

GOD TELLS HIS PEOPLE THE DAY AND HOUR OF JESUS' COMING.—The voice of God is heard from heaven, declaring the day and hour of Jesus' coming, and delivering the everlasting covenant to His people. Like peals of loudest thunder His words roll through the earth. The Israel of God stand listening, with their eyes fixed upward. Their countenances are lighted up with His glory, and shine as did the face of Moses when he came down from Sinai. The wicked cannot look upon them. And when the blessing is pronounced on those who have honored God by keeping His Sabbath holy, there is a mighty shout of victory.—GC 640.

5

Christ's Second Coming

A SMALL, BLACK CLOUD IS THE SIGN OF JESUS' COMING.—Soon there appears in the east a small black cloud, about half the size of a man's hand. It is the cloud which surrounds the Saviour and which seems in the distance to be shrouded in darkness. The people of God know this to be the sign of the Son of man. In solemn silence they gaze upon it as it draws nearer the earth, becoming lighter and more glorious, until it is a great white cloud, its base a glory like consuming fire, and above it the rainbow of the covenant. Jesus rides forth as a mighty conqueror.—GC 640, 641.

Soon our eyes were drawn to the east, for a small black cloud had appeared, about half as large as a man's hand, which we all knew was the sign of the Son of man. In solemn silence we all gazed on the cloud as it drew nearer, and became lighter, glorious, and still more glorious, till it was a great white cloud. The bottom appeared like fire; a rainbow was over the cloud, while around it were ten thousand angels, singing a most lovely song; and upon it sat the Son of man. His hair was white and curly and lay on His shoulders, and upon His head were many crowns. His feet had the appearance of fire; in His right hand was a sharp sickle, in His left a silver trumpet. His eyes were as a flame of fire, which searched His children through and through.—1T 60.

WHOLE WORLD WILL SEE.—"For as the lightning cometh out of the east, and shineth even unto the west; so shall also the coming of the Son of man be." Matthew 24:24-27, 31; 25:31; Revelation 1:7; 1 Thessalonians 4:16, 17. This coming there is no possibility of counterfeiting. It will be universally known—witnessed by the whole world.—GC 625.

JESUS RETURNS IN GLORY SURROUNDED BY A CLOUD OF ANGELS.—With anthems of celestial melody the holy angels, a vast unnumbered throng, attend Him on His way. The firmament seems filled with radiant forms—"ten thousand times ten thousand, and thousands of thousands." No human pen can portray the scene; no mortal mind is adequate to conceive its splendor. . . . As the living cloud comes still nearer, every eye beholds the Prince of life. No crown of thorns now mars that sacred head; but a diadem of glory rests on His holy brow. His countenance outshines the dazzling brightness of the noonday sun. . . .

The King of kings descends upon the cloud, wrapped in flaming fire. The heavens are rolled together as a scroll, the earth trembles before Him, and every mountain and island is moved out of its place. "Our God shall come, and shall not keep silence: a fire shall devour before Him, and it shall be very tempestuous round about Him. He shall call to the heavens from above, and to the earth, that He may judge His people." Psalm 50:3, 4.—GC 641, 642.

JESUS CLEARLY SEEN ON THE CLOUD.—The living cloud of majesty, and unsurpassed glory, came still nearer, and we could clearly behold the lovely person of Jesus. He did not wear a crown of thorns; but a crown of glory decked his holy brow. Upon his vesture and thigh was a name written, KING OF KINGS AND LORD OF LORDS. His eyes were as a flame of fire, his feet had the appearance of fine brass, and his voice sounded like many musical instruments. His countenance was as bright as the noon-day sun.—1SG 207.

JOY OF GOD'S PEOPLE.—The revelation of His own glory in the form of humanity will bring heaven so near to men that the beauty adorning the inner temple will be seen in every soul in whom the Saviour dwells. Men will be captivated by the glory of an abiding Christ. And in currents of praise and thanksgiving from the many souls thus won to God, glory will flow back to the great Giver.

"Arise, shine; for thy light is come, and the glory of the Lord is risen upon thee." Isaiah 60:1. To those who go out to meet the Bridegroom is this message given. Christ is coming with power and great glory. He is coming with His own glory and with the glory of the Father. He is coming with all the holy angels with Him. While all the world is plunged in darkness, there will be light in every dwelling of the saints. They will catch the first light of His second appearing. The unsullied light will shine from His splendor, and Christ the Redeemer will be admired by all who have served Him. While the wicked flee from His presence, Christ's followers will rejoice. The patriarch Job, looking down to the time of Christ's second advent, said, "Whom I shall see for myself, and mine eyes shall behold, and not a stranger." Job 19:27, margin.

To His faithful followers Christ has been a daily companion and familiar friend. They have lived in close contact, in constant communion with God. Upon them the glory of the Lord has risen. In them the light of the knowledge of the glory of God in the face of Jesus Christ has been reflected. Now they rejoice in the undimmed rays of the brightness and glory of the King in His majesty. They are prepared for the communion of heaven; for they have heaven in their hearts.

With uplifted heads, with the bright beams of the Sun of Righteousness shining upon them, with rejoicing that their redemption draweth nigh, they go forth to meet the Bridegroom, saying, "Lo, this is our God; we have waited for Him, and He will save us." Isaiah 25:9.

"And I heard as it were the voice of a great multitude, and as the voice of many waters, and as the voice of mighty thunderings, saying, Alleluia; for the Lord God omnipotent reigneth. Let us be glad and rejoice, and give honour to Him; for the marriage of the Lamb is come, and His wife hath made herself ready. . . . And he saith unto me, Write, Blessed are they which are called unto the marriage supper of the Lamb." "He is Lord of lords, and King of kings; and they that are with Him are called, and chosen, and faithful." Revelation 19:6-9; 17:14.—COL 420, 421.

RIGHTEOUS DEAD AND LIVING WILL SEE JESUS TO-GETHER.—Paul showed that those living when Christ should come would not go to meet their Lord in advance of those who had fallen asleep in Jesus. The voice of the Archangel and the trump of God would reach the sleeping ones, and the dead in Christ should rise first, before the touch of immortality should be given to the living. "Then we which are alive and remain shall be caught up together with them in the clouds, to meet the Lord in the air: and so shall we ever be with the Lord. Wherefore comfort one another with these words" [1 Thessalonians 4:17, 18].—AA 258.

GARMENTS OF WHITEST WHITE.—Christ emptied Himself, and took the form of a servant, and offered sacrifice, Himself the priest, Himself the victim. As the high priest, after performing his service in the holy of holies, came forth to the waiting congregation in his pontifical robes, so Christ will come the second time clothed in glorious garments of the whitest white, "such as no fuller on earth can whiten them." He will come in His own glory, and in the glory of His Father, as King of kings and Lord of lords, and all the angelic host will escort Him on His way.—Ms 113, 1899 quoted in 1BC 1111, 1112.

JESUS RAISES THE SLEEPING SAINTS TO IMMORTAL LIFE.— Amid the reeling of the earth, the flashing of lightning, and the roaring of thunder, the voice of the Son of God calls forth the sleeping saints. He looks upon the graves of the righteous, then raising His hands to heaven He cries, "Awake, awake, awake, ye that sleep in the dust, and arise!" Throughout the length and breadth of the earth, the dead shall hear that voice, and they that hear shall live. And the whole earth shall ring with the tread of the exceeding great army of every nation, kindred, tongue, and people. From the prison-house of death they come, clothed with immortal glory, crying, "O death, where is thy sting? O grave, where is thy victory?" [1 Corinthians 15:55.] And the living righteous and the risen saints unite their voices in a long, glad shout of victory.

All come forth from their graves the same in stature as when they entered the tomb. Adam, who stands among the risen throng, is of lofty height and majestic form, in stature but little below the Son of God. He presents a marked contrast to the people of later generations; in this one respect is shown the great degeneracy of the race. But all arise from their last deep slumber with the freshness and vigor of eternal youth. In the beginning, man was created in the likeness of God, not only in character, but in form and feature. Sin defaced and almost obliterated the divine image; but Christ came to restore that which had been lost. He will change our vile bodies, and fashion them like unto His glorious body. The mortal, corruptible form, devoid of comeliness, once polluted with sin, becomes perfect, beautiful, and immortal. All blemishes and deformities are left in the grave. The redeemed bear the image of their Lord. Oh, wonderful redemption! long talked of, long hoped for, contemplated with eager anticipation, but never fully understood.—4SP 463, 464.

First Thought of the Resurrected.—As they [the righteous] are called forth from their deep slumber they begin to think just where they ceased. The last sensation was the pang of death; the last thought, that they were falling beneath the power of the grave. When they arise from the tomb, their first glad thought will be echoed in the triumphal shout: "O death, where is thy sting? O grave, where is thy victory?" [1 Corinthians 15:55].—GC 550.

Death Is a Small Matter.—To the believer, Christ is the resurrection and the life. In our Saviour the life that was lost through sin is restored; for He has life in Himself to quicken whom He will. He is invested with the right to give immortality. The life that He laid down in humanity, He takes up again, and gives to humanity. "I am come," He said, "that they might have life, and that they might have it more abundantly." "Whosoever drinketh of the water that I shall give him shall never thirst; but the water that I shall give him shall be in him a well of water springing up into everlasting life." "Whoso eateth My flesh, and drinketh My blood, hath eternal life; and I will raise him up at the last day." John 10:10; 4:14; 6:54.

To the believer, death is but a small matter. Christ speaks of it as if it were of little moment. "If a man keep My saying, he shall never see death," "he shall never taste of death." To the Christian, death is but a sleep, a moment of silence and darkness. The life is hid with Christ in God, and "when Christ, who is our life, shall appear, then shall ye also appear with Him in glory." John 8:51, 52; Colossians 3:4.

The voice that cried from the cross, "It is finished," was

heard among the dead. It pierced the walls of sepulchers, and summoned the sleepers to arise. Thus will it be when the voice of Christ shall be heard from heaven. That voice will penetrate the graves and unbar the tombs, and the dead in Christ shall arise. At the Saviour's resurrection a few graves were opened, but at His second coming all the precious dead shall hear His voice, and shall come forth to glorious, immortal life. The same power that raised Christ from the dead will raise His church, and glorify it with Him, above all principalities, above all powers, above every name that is named, not only in this world, but also in the world to come.—DA 786, 787.

CHILDREN RESTORED—His faithful ones [will] be rewarded, when, at His coming, death loses its sting and the grave is robbed of the victory it has claimed. Then will He restore to His servants the children that have been taken from them by death. "Thus saith the Lord; A voice was heard in Ramah, lamentation, and bitter weeping; Rachel weeping for her children refused to be comforted for her children, because they were not. Thus saith the Lord; Refrain thy voice from weeping, and thine eyes from tears: for thy work shall be rewarded . . . and they shall come again from the land of the enemy. And there is hope in thine end, saith the Lord, that thy children shall come again to their own border." Jeremiah 31:15-17.—PK 239.

SLEEPING SAINTS GUARDED AS PRECIOUS JEWELS.—The Life-giver will call up His purchased possession in the first resurrection, and until that triumphant hour, when the last trump shall sound and the vast army shall come forth to eternal victory, every sleeping saint will be kept in safety and will be guarded as a precious jewel, who is known to God by name. By the power of the Saviour that dwelt in them while living and because they were partakers of the divine nature, they are brought forth from the dead.—Letter 65a, 1894 quoted in 4BC 1143.

WE WILL KNOW OUR FRIENDS.—The resurrection of Jesus was a type of the final resurrection of all who sleep in Him. The countenance of the risen Saviour, His manner, His speech, were all familiar to His disciples. As Jesus arose from the dead, so those who sleep in Him are to rise again. We shall know our friends, even as the disciples knew Jesus. They may have been deformed, diseased, or disfigured, in this mortal life, and they rise in perfect health and symmetry; yet in the glorified body their identity will be perfectly preserved. Then shall we know even as also we are known. 1 Corinthians 13:12. In the face radiant with the light shining from the face of Jesus, we shall recognize the lineaments of those we love.—DA 804.

WE WILL KNOW ONE ANOTHER.—God's greatest gift is Christ, whose life is ours, given for us. He died for us, and was raised for us, that we might come forth from the tomb to a glorious companionship with heavenly angels, to meet our loved ones and to recognize their faces, for the Christlikeness does not destroy their image, but transforms it into His glorious image. Every saint connected in family relationship here will know each other there.—Letter 79, 1898 quoted in 3SM 316.

PERSONALITY PRESERVED IN A NEW BODY.—Our personal identity is preserved in the resurrection, though not the same particles of matter or material substance as went into the grave. The wondrous works of God are a mystery to man. The spirit, the character of man, is returned to God, there to be preserved. In the resurrection every man will have his own character. God in His own time will call forth the dead, giving again the breath of life, and bidding the dry bones live. The same form will come forth, but it will be free from disease and every defect. It lives again bearing the same individuality of features, so that friend will recognize friend. There is no law of God in nature which shows that God gives back the same identical particles of matter which composed the body before death. God shall give the righteous dead a body that will please Him.

Paul illustrates this subject by the kernel of grain sown in the field. The planted kernel decays, but there comes forth a new kernel. The natural substance in the grain that decays is never raised as before, but God giveth it a body as it hath pleased Him. A much finer material will compose the human body, for it is a new creation, a new birth. It is sown a natural body, it is raised a spiritual body.—Ms 76, 1900 quoted in 6BC 1093.

CLOSENESS BETWEEN GOD AND RESURRECTED SAINTS.— Christ declared to His hearers that if there were no resurrection of the dead, the Scriptures which they professed to believe would be of no avail. He said, "But as touching the resurrection of the dead, have ye not read that which was spoken unto you by God, saying, I am the God of Abraham, and the God of Isaac, and the God of Jacob? God is not the God of the dead, but of the living." God counts the things that are not as though they were. He sees the end from the beginning, and beholds the result of His work as though it were now accomplished. The precious dead, from Adam down to the last saint who dies, will hear the voice of the Son of God, and will come forth from the grave to immortal life. God will be their God, and they shall be His people. There will be a close and tender relationship between God and the risen saints. This condition, which is anticipated in His purpose, He beholds as if it were already existing. The dead live unto Him.—DA 606.

RAISED TO ONENESS WITH CHRIST.—He [the believer] may die, as Christ died, but the life of the Saviour is in him. His life is hid with Christ in God. "I am come that they might have life," Jesus said, "and that they might have it more abundantly." He carries on the great process by which believers are made one with Him in this present life, to be one with Him throughout all eternity.

At the last day He will raise them as a part of Himself. . . . Christ became one with us in order that we might become one with Him in divinity.—RH June 18, 1901 quoted in Mar 301.

AWAKENED TO DIE NO MORE.—Ministering angels are round about us giving us to drink of the water of life to refresh our souls in the closing scenes of life. There is a pledge from Him who is the resurrection and the life, that those who sleep in Jesus will Christ bring with Him from the grave. The trump will sound, the dead will awaken to life, to die no more. The eternal morning has come to them, for there will be no night in the city of God.—Letter 78, 1890 quoted in 2SM 250.

THE FINISHING TOUCH OF IMMORTALITY.—The Life-giver is coming to break the fetters of the tomb. He is to bring forth the captives and proclaim, "I am the resurrection and the life." There stands the risen host. The last thought was of death and its pangs. The last thoughts they had were of the grave and the tomb, but now they proclaim, "O death, where is thy sting? O grave, where is thy victory?" The pangs of death were the last things they felt. "O death, where is thy sting?" The last thing they acknowledged was the pangs of death. When they awake the pain is all gone. . . .

Here they stand, and the finishing touch of immortality is put upon them, and they go up to meet their Lord in the air. The gates of the city of God swing back upon their hinges, and the nations that have kept the truth enter in. There are the columns of angels on either side, and the ransomed of God walk in through the cherubims and seraphims. Christ bids them welcome and puts upon them His benediction. "Well done, thou good and faithful servant: . . . enter thou into the joy of thy Lord." What is that joy? He sees of the travail of His soul, and is satisfied.

That is what we labor for. Here is one, who in the night season we pleaded with God on his behalf. There is one that we talked with on his dying bed, and he hung his helpless soul upon Jesus. Here is one who was a poor drunkard. We tried to get his eyes fixed upon Him who is mighty to save and we told him that Christ could give him the victory. There are the crowns of immortal glory upon their heads, and then the redeemed cast their glittering crowns at the feet of Jesus.—Ms 18, 1894 quoted in 6BC 1093.

RIGHTEOUS DEAD AND LIVING SEE JESUS TOGETHER.— In his first epistle to the Thessalonian believers, Paul endeavored to instruct them regarding the true state of the dead. He spoke of those who die as being asleep—in a state of unconsciousness: "I would not have you to be ignorant, brethren, concerning them which are asleep, that ye sorrow not, even as others which have no hope. For if we believe that Jesus died and rose again, even so them also which sleep in Jesus will God bring with Him. . . . For the Lord Himself shall descend from heaven with a shout, with the voice of the Archangel, and with the trump of God: and the dead in Christ shall rise first: then we which are alive and remain shall be caught up together with them in the clouds, to meet the Lord in the air: and so shall we ever be with the Lord."

The Thessalonians had eagerly grasped the idea that Christ was coming to change the faithful who were alive, and to take them to Himself. They had carefully guarded the lives of their friends, lest they should die and lose the blessing which they looked forward to receiving at the coming of their Lord. But one after another their loved ones had been taken from them, and with anguish the Thessalonians had looked for the last time upon the faces of their dead, hardly daring to hope to meet them in a future life.

As Paul's epistle was opened and read, great joy and consolation was brought to the church by the words revealing the true state of the dead. Paul showed that those living when Christ should come would not go to meet their Lord in advance of those who had fallen asleep in Jesus. The voice of the Archangel and the trump of God would reach the sleeping ones, and the dead in Christ should rise first, before the touch of immortality should be given to the living. "Then we which are alive and remain shall be caught up together with them in the clouds, to meet the Lord in the air: and so shall we ever be with the Lord. Wherefore comfort one another with these words."—AA 257, 258.

THE FUTURE KINGDOM IN MINIATURE.—Moses upon the mount of transfiguration was a witness to Christ's victory over sin and death. He represented those who shall come forth from the grave at the resurrection of the just. Elijah, who had been translated to heaven without seeing death, represented those who will be living upon the earth at Christ's second coming, and who will be "changed, in a moment, in the twinkling of an eye, at the last trump;" when "this mortal must put on immortality," and "this corruptible must put on incorruption." 1 Corinthians 15:51-53. Jesus was clothed with the light of heaven, as He will appear when He shall come "the second time without sin unto salvation." For He will come "in the glory of His Father with the holy angels." Hebrews 9:28; Mark 8:38. The Saviour's promise to the disciples was now fulfilled. Upon the mount the future kingdom of glory was represented in miniature—Christ the King, Moses a representative of the risen saints, and Elijah of the translated ones.—DA 421, 422.

LINES PENNED ON THE DEATH OF MRS. WHITE'S NIECE.—Our fondest hopes are often blighted here. Our loved ones are torn from us by death. We close their eyes and habit them for the tomb, and lay them away from our sight. But hope bears our spirits up. We are not parted forever, but shall meet the loved ones who sleep in Jesus. They shall come again from the land of the enemy. The Life-giver is coming. Myriads of holy angels escort Him on His way. He bursts the bands of death, breaks the fetters of the tomb, the precious captives come forth in health and immortal beauty.

As the little infants come forth immortal from their dusty beds, they immediately wing their way to their mothers' arms. They meet again nevermore to part. But many of the little ones have no mother there. We listen in vain for the rapturous song of triumph from the mother. The angels receive the motherless infants and conduct them to the tree of life.

Jesus places the golden ring of light, the crown upon their little heads. God grant that the dear mother of "Eva" may be there, that her little wings may be folded upon the glad bosom of her mother.—YI April, 1858 quoted in 2SM 259, 260.

FAMILIES AND FRIENDS REUNITED.—The living righteous are changed "in a moment, in the twinkling of an eye." At the voice of God they were glorified; now they are made immortal and with the risen saints are caught up to meet their Lord in the air. Angels "gather together His elect from the four winds, from one end of heaven to the other." Little children are borne by holy angels to their mothers' arms. Friends long separated by death are united, nevermore to part, and with songs of gladness ascend together to the City of God.

On each side of the cloudy chariot are wings, and beneath it are living wheels; and as the chariot rolls upward, the wheels cry, "Holy," and the wings, as they move, cry, "Holy," and the retinue of angels cry, "Holy, holy, holy, Lord God Almighty." And the redeemed shout, "Alleluia!" as the chariot moves onward toward the New Jerusalem.—GC 645.

THE WICKED UNSUCCESSFULLY ATTEMPT TO HIDE FROM JESUS.—The wicked pray to be covered by the rocks of the mountains, rather than meet the face of Him whom they have despised and rejected. . . .

Those who derided His [Jesus'] claim to be the Son of God are speechless now. There is the haughty Herod who jeered at His royal title, and bade the mocking soldiers crown Him king. There are the very men who with impious hands placed upon His form the purple robe, upon His sacred brow the thorny crown, and in His unresisting hand the mimic scepter, and bowed before Him in blasphemous mockery. The men who smote and spit upon the Prince of life, now turn from His piercing gaze, and seek to flee from the overpowering glory of His presence. Those who drove the nails through His hands and feet, the soldier who pierced His side, behold these marks with terror and remorse.

With awful distinctness do priests and rulers recall the events of Calvary. With shuddering horror they remember how, wagging their heads in Satanic exultation, they exclaimed, "He saved others; himself he cannot save. If he be the King of Israel, let him now come down from the cross, and we will believe him. He trusted in God; let him deliver him now, if he will have him." [Matthew 27:42, 43.] . . .

And now there rises a cry of mortal agony. Louder than the shout, "Crucify him! crucify him!" which rang through the streets of Jerusalem, swells the awful, despairing wail, "He is the Son of God! He is the true Messiah!" They seek to flee from the presence of the King of kings. In the deep caverns of the earth, rent asunder by the warring of the elements, they vainly attempt to hide.—4SP 460-462.

REDEEMED TAKE SEVEN DAYS TRAVELING TO HEAVEN.—
We all entered the cloud together, and were seven days ascending to the sea of glass, when Jesus brought the crowns, and with His own right hand placed them on our heads. He gave us harps of gold and palms of victory. Here on the sea of glass the 144,000 stood in a perfect square. Some of them had very bright crowns, others not so bright. Some crowns appeared heavy with stars, while others had but few. All were perfectly satisfied with their crowns. And they were all clothed with a glorious white mantle from their shoulders to their feet. Angels were all about us as we marched over the sea of glass to the gate of the city. Jesus raised His mighty, glorious arm, laid hold of the pearly gate, swung it back on its glittering hinges, and said to us, "You have washed your robes in My blood, stood stiffly for My truth, enter in." We all marched in and felt that we had a perfect right in the city.—LS 66, 67.

Jesus Welcomes the Redeemed to the New Jerusalem.—Before the ransomed throng is the Holy City. Jesus opens wide the pearly gates, and the nations that have kept the truth enter in. There they behold the Paradise of God, the home of Adam in his innocency. Then that voice, richer than any music that ever fell on mortal ear, is heard, saying: "Your conflict is ended." "Come, ye blessed of My Father, inherit the kingdom prepared for you from the foundation of the world."

Now is fulfilled the Saviour's prayer for His disciples: "I will that they also, whom Thou hast given Me, be with Me where I am." "Faultless before the presence of His glory with exceeding joy" (Jude 24), Christ presents to the Father the purchase of His blood, declaring: "Here am I, and the children whom Thou hast given Me." "Those that Thou gavest Me I have kept."

Oh, the wonders of redeeming love! the rapture of that hour when the infinite Father, looking upon the ransomed, shall behold His image, sin's discord banished, its blight removed, and the human once more in harmony with the divine!

With unutterable love, Jesus welcomes His faithful ones to the joy of their Lord. The Saviour's joy is in seeing, in the kingdom of glory, the souls that have been saved by His agony and humiliation. And the redeemed will be sharers in His joy, as they behold, among the blessed, those who have been won to Christ through their prayers, their labors, and their loving sacrifice. As they gather about the great white throne, gladness unspeakable will fill their hearts, when they behold those whom they have won for

Christ, and see that one has gained others, and these still others, all brought into the haven of rest, there to lay their crowns at Jesus' feet and praise Him through the endless cycles of eternity.—GC 646, 647.

THE TWO ADAMS MEET IN THE HOLY CITY.—As the ransomed ones are welcomed to the City of God, there rings out upon the air an exultant cry of adoration. The two Adams are about to meet. The Son of God is standing with outstretched arms to receive the father of our race—the being whom He created, who sinned against his Maker, and for whose sin the marks of the crucifixion are borne upon the Saviour's form. As Adam discerns the prints of the cruel nails, he does not fall upon the bosom of his Lord, but in humiliation casts himself at His feet, crying: "Worthy, worthy is the Lamb that was slain!" Tenderly the Saviour lifts him up and bids him look once more upon the Eden home from which he has so long been exiled.

After his expulsion from Eden, Adam's life on earth was filled with sorrow. Every dying leaf, every victim of sacrifice, every blight upon the fair face of nature, every stain upon man's purity, was a fresh reminder of his sin. Terrible was the agony of remorse as he beheld iniquity abounding, and, in answer to his warnings, met the reproaches cast upon himself as the cause of sin. With patient humility he bore, for nearly a thousand years, the penalty of transgression. Faithfully did he repent of his sin and trust in the merits of the promised Saviour, and he died in the hope of a resurrection. The Son of God redeemed man's failure and fall; and now, through the work of the atonement, Adam is reinstated in his first dominion.

Transported with joy, he beholds the trees that were once his delight—the very trees whose fruit he himself had gathered in the days of his innocence and joy. He sees the vines that his own hands have trained, the very flowers that he once loved to care for. His mind grasps the reality of the scene; he comprehends that this is indeed Eden restored, more lovely now than when he was banished from it. The Saviour leads him to the tree of life and plucks the glorious fruit and bids him eat. He looks about him and beholds a multitude of his family redeemed, standing in the Paradise of God. Then he casts his glittering crown at the feet of Jesus and, falling upon His breast, embraces the Redeemer. He touches the golden harp, and the vaults of heaven echo the triumphant song: "Worthy, worthy, worthy is the Lamb that was slain, and lives again!" The family of Adam take up the strain and cast their crowns at the Saviour's feet as they bow before Him in adoration.

This reunion is witnessed by the angels who wept at the fall of Adam and rejoiced when Jesus, after His resurrection, ascended to heaven, having opened the grave for all who should believe on His name. Now they behold the work of redemption accomplished, and they unite their voices in the song of praise.—GC 647, 648.

STANDING WITH THE LAMB UPON THE SEA OF GLASS.— Upon the crystal sea before the throne, that sea of glass as it were mingled with fire—so resplendent is it with the glory of God—are gathered the company that have "gotten the victory over the beast, and over his image, and over his mark, and over the number of his name." With the Lamb upon Mount Zion, "having the harps of God," they stand, the hundred and forty and four thousand that were redeemed from among men; and there is heard, as the sound of many waters, and as the sound of a great thunder, "the voice of harpers harping with their harps." And they sing "a new song" before the throne, a song which no man can learn save the hundred and forty and four thousand. It is the song of Moses and the Lamb—a song of deliverance.

None but the hundred and forty-four thousand can learn that song; for it is the song of their experience—an experience such as no other company have ever had. "These are they which follow the Lamb whithersoever He goeth." These, having been translated from the earth, from among the living, are counted as "the first fruits unto God and to the Lamb." Revelation 15:2, 3; 14:1-5. "These are they which came out of great tribulation;" they have passed through the time of trouble such as never was since there was a nation; they have endured the anguish of the time of Jacob's trouble; they have stood without an intercessor through the final outpouring of God's judgments. But they have been delivered, for they have "washed their robes, and made them white in the blood of the Lamb." "In their mouth was found no guile: for they are without fault" before God. "Therefore are they before the throne of God, and serve Him day and night in His temple: and He that sitteth on the throne shall dwell among them."

They have seen the earth wasted with famine and pestilence, the sun having power to scorch men with great heat, and they themselves have endured suffering, hunger, and thirst. But "they shall hunger no more, neither thirst any more; neither shall the sun light on them, nor any heat. For the Lamb which is in the midst of the throne shall feed them, and shall lead them unto living fountains of waters: and God shall wipe away all tears from their eyes." Revelation 7:14-17.—GC 648, 649.

6

Our Eternal Inheritance

IMMORTAL INHERITANCE.—Language fails to express the value of the immortal inheritance. The glory, riches, and honor offered by the Son of God are of such infinite value that it is beyond the power of men or even angels to give any just idea of their worth, their excellence, their magnificence. If men, plunged in sin and degradation, refuse these heavenly benefits, refuse a life of obedience, trample upon the gracious invitations of mercy, and choose the paltry things of earth because they are seen, and it is convenient for their present enjoyment to pursue a course of sin, Jesus will carry out the figure in the parable; such shall not taste of His glory, but the invitation will be extended to another class.—2T 40.

INHERITORS AT LAST.—Not until the personal advent of Christ can His people receive the kingdom. . . . Man in his present state is mortal, corruptible; but the kingdom of God will be incorruptible, enduring forever. Therefore man in his present state cannot enter into the kingdom of God. But when Jesus comes, He confers immortality upon His people; and then He calls them to inherit the kingdom of which they have hitherto been only heirs.—GC 322, 323.

LIFE INSURANCE.—Through the agency of the Holy Spirit, God works a moral change in the lives of His people, changing them into the likeness of Christ. Then, when the last trumpet call shall reach the ears of the dead who sleep in Christ, they will come forth to a new life, clothed with the garments of salvation. They enter in through the gates into the City of God, welcomed to the happiness and joy of their Lord. Would that we all could understand and ever keep in mind the joys that await those who keep their eyes on the pattern Christ Jesus, and in this life seek to form a character like His.

The Word of God contains our life insurance policy. To eat the flesh and drink the blood of the Son of God means to study the Word and to carry that Word into the life in obedience to all its precepts. Those who thus partake of the Son of God become partakers of the divine nature, one with Christ. They breathe a holy atmosphere, in which only the soul can truly live. They carry in their lives an assurance of the holy principles received from the Word—their lives are worked by the power of the Holy Spirit, and they have an earnest of the immortality that will be theirs through the death and resurrection of Christ. Should the earthly body decay, the principles of their faith sustain them, for they are partakers of the divine nature. Because Christ was raised from the dead, they grasp the pledge of their resurrection, and eternal life is their reward.

This truth is an eternal truth, because Christ Himself taught it. He has engaged to raise the righteous dead, for He gave His life for the life of the world. "As the living Father hath sent me, and I live by the Father: so he that eateth me, even he shall live by me" (John 6:57). "I am the bread of life: he that cometh to me shall never hunger" (verse 35).—Letter 82, 1907 quoted in UL 78.

MANSIONS PREPARED FOR REDEEMED.—How great will be the joy when the redeemed of the Lord shall all meet—gathered into the mansions prepared for them! Oh, what rejoicing for all who have been impartial, unselfish laborers together with God in carrying forward His work in the earth! What satisfaction will every reaper have, when the clear, musical voice of Jesus shall be heard, saying, "Come, ye blessed of My Father, inherit the kingdom prepared for you from the foundation of the world." "Enter thou into the joy of thy Lord."—RH October 10, 1907 quoted in CS 348.

TITLE TO THE KINGDOM.—We have His promise. We hold the title deeds to real estate in the kingdom of glory. Never were title deeds drawn up more strictly according to law, or signed more legibly, than those that give God's people a right to the heavenly mansions. "Let not your heart be troubled," Christ says: "ye believe in God, believe also in me. In my Father's house are many mansions: if it were not so, I would have told you. I go to prepare a place for you. And if I go and prepare a place for you, I will come again, and receive you unto myself; that where I am, there ye may be also." (John 14:1-3)—Letter 144, 1903 quoted in TDG 202.

CROWNS FOR THE FAITHFUL.—When the Lord makes up His jewels, the true, the frank, the honest, will be looked upon with pleasure. Angels are employed in making crowns for such ones, and upon these star-gemmed crowns will be reflected, with splendor, the light which radiates from the throne of God.

Talk of heavenly things. Talk of Jesus, His loveliness and glory, and of His undying love for you, and let your heart flow out in love and gratitude to Him, who died to save you. O, get ready to meet your Lord in peace. Those who are ready will soon receive an unfading crown of life, and will dwell forever in the kingdom of God, with Christ, with angels, and with those who have been redeemed by the precious blood of Christ.

A crown of glory . . . is laid up for us who wait, and love, and long for, the appearing of the Saviour.

It is the waiting ones who are to be crowned with glory, honor, and immortality. You need not talk . . . of the honors of the world, or the praise of its great ones. They are all vanity. Let but the finger of God touch them, and they would soon go back to dust again. I want honor that is lasting, honor that is immortal, honor that will never perish; a crown that is richer than any crown that ever decked the brow of a monarch.

In that day the redeemed will shine forth in the glory of the Father and His Son. The angels of heaven, touching their golden harps, will welcome the King, and those who are the trophies of His victory—those who have been washed and made white in the blood of the Lamb. A song of triumph will peal forth, filling all heaven. Christ has conquered. He enters the heavenly courts accompanied by His redeemed ones, the witnesses that His mission of suffering and self-sacrifice has not been in vain. . . .

I saw a very great number of angels bring from the city glorious crowns—a crown for every saint, with his name written thereon. As Jesus called for the crowns, angels presented them to Him, and with His own right hand the lovely Jesus placed the crowns on the heads of the saints. In the same manner the angels brought the harps, and Jesus presented them also to the saints. The commanding angels first struck the note, and then every voice was raised in grateful, happy praise, and every hand skillfully swept over the strings of the harp, sending forth melodious music in rich and perfect strains. . . .

Within the city there was everything to feast the eye. Rich glory they beheld everywhere. Then Jesus looked upon His redeemed saints; their countenances were radiant with glory; and as He fixed His loving eyes upon them, He said, with His rich, musical voice, "I behold the travail of My soul, and am satisfied. This rich glory is yours to enjoy eternally. Your sorrows are ended. There shall be no more death, neither sorrow nor crying, neither shall there be any more pain." . . .

I then saw Jesus leading His people to the tree of life. . . . Upon the tree of life was most beautiful fruit, of which the saints could partake freely; in the city was a most glorious throne, from which proceeded a pure river of water of life, clear as crystal. On each side of this river was the tree of life, and on the banks of the river were other beautiful trees bearing fruit. . . .

Language is altogether too feeble to attempt a description of heaven. As the scene rises before me, I am lost in amazement. Carried away with the surpassing splendor and excellent glory, I lay down the pen, and exclaim, "Oh, what love! what wondrous love!" The most exalted language fails to describe the glory of heaven or the matchless depths of a Saviour's love.—Mar 309, 310.

RICH ROBES AND GLORIOUS CROWNS.—The heirs of God have come from garrets, from hovels, from dungeons, from scaffolds, from mountains, from deserts, from the caves of the earth, from the caverns of the sea. But they are no longer feeble, afflicted, scattered, and oppressed. Henceforth they are to be ever with the Lord. They stand before the throne clad in richer robes than the most honored of the earth have ever worn. They are crowned with diadems more glorious than were ever placed upon the brow of earthly monarchs. The days of pain and weeping are forever ended. The King of glory has wiped the tears from all faces; every cause of grief has been removed. Amid the waving of palm-branches they pour forth a song of praise, clear, sweet, and harmonious; every voice takes up the strain, until the anthem swells through the vaults of Heaven.—4SP 467.

CROWNS, HARPS, AND PALM BRANCHES.—Before entering the City of God, the Saviour bestows upon His followers the emblems of victory and invests them with the insignia of their royal state. The glittering ranks are drawn up in the form of a hollow square about their King, whose form rises in majesty high above saint and angel, whose countenance beams upon them full of benignant love. Throughout the unnumbered host of the redeemed every glance is fixed upon Him, every eye beholds His glory whose "visage was so marred more than any man, and His form more than the sons of men." Upon the heads of the overcomers, Jesus with His own right hand places the crown of glory. For each there is a crown, bearing his own "new name" (Revelation 2:17), and the inscription, "Holiness to the Lord." In every hand are placed the victor's palm and the shining harp. Then, as the commanding angels strike the note, every hand sweeps the harp strings with skillful touch, awaking sweet music in rich, melodious strains. Rapture unutterable thrills every heart, and each voice is raised in grateful praise: "Unto Him that loved us, and washed us from our sins in His own blood, and hath made us kings and priests unto God and His Father; to Him be glory and dominion for ever and ever." Revelation 1:5, 6.—GC 645, 646.

7

A Heavenly Atmosphere

THE CHRISTIAN'S SUMMER.—This earth is the place of preparation for heaven. The time spent here is the Christian's winter. Here the chilly winds of affliction blow upon us, and the waves of trouble roll against us. But in the near future, when Christ comes, sorrow and sighing will be forever ended. Then will be the Christian's summer. All trials will be over, and there will be no more sickness or death. "God shall wipe away all tears from their eyes; and there shall be no more death, neither sorrow, nor crying . . . : for the former things are passed away."—Ms 28, 1886 quoted in 7BC 988.

TRIALS CANNOT BE RECALLED.—We tried to call up our greatest trials, but they looked so small compared with the far more exceeding and eternal weight of glory that surrounded us, that we could not speak them out, and we all cried out, Alleluia! heaven is cheap enough, and we touched our golden harps and made heaven's arches ring.—2SG 34, 35.

A HAPPY FAMILY.—The nations of the saved will know no other law than the law of heaven. All will be a happy, united family, clothed with the garments of praise and thanksgiving. Over the scene the morning stars will sing together, and the sons of God will shout for joy, while God and Christ will unite in proclaiming, "There shall be no more sin, neither shall there be any more death."—PK 732, 733.

REALIZATION GREATER THAN EXPECTATION.—Christ accepted humanity, and lived on this earth a pure, sanctified life. For this reason He has received the appointment of judge. He who occupies the position of judge is God manifest in the flesh. What a joy it will be to recognize in Him our Teacher and Redeemer, bearing still the marks of the crucifixion, from which shine beams of glory, giving additional value to the crowns which the redeemed receive from His hands, the very hands outstretched in blessing over His disciples as He ascended. The very voice which said, "Lo, I am with you alway, even unto the end of the world," bids His ransomed ones welcome to His presence.

The very One who gave His precious life for them, who by His grace moved their hearts to repentance, who awakened them to their need of repentance, receives them now into His joy. Oh, how they love Him! The realization of their hope is infinitely greater than their expectation. Their joy is complete, and they take their glittering crowns and cast them at their Redeemer's feet.—RH June 18, 1901 quoted in CS 349.

GOD HAS NOT REVEALED ALL.—The Lord has made every provision for our happiness in the future life, but He has made no revelations regarding these plans, and we are not to speculate concerning them. Neither are we to measure the conditions of the future life by the conditions of this life.

Matters of vital importance have been plainly revealed in the Word of God. These subjects are worthy of our deepest thought. But we are not to search into matters on which God has been silent. Some have put forth the speculation that the redeemed will not have gray hair. Other foolish suppositions have been put forward, as though these were matters of importance. May God help His people to think rationally. When questions arise upon which we are uncertain, we should ask, "What saith the Scripture?"—Ms 28, 1904 quoted in 1SM 173.

JESUS WILL EXPLAIN.—Long have we waited for our Saviour's return. But none the less sure is the promise. Soon we shall be in our promised home. There Jesus will lead us beside the living stream flowing from the throne of God, and will explain to us the dark providences through which He led us in order to perfect our characters. There we shall see on every hand the beautiful trees of Paradise, in the midst of them the tree of life. There we shall behold with undimmed vision the beauties of Eden restored. There we shall cast at the feet of our Redeemer the crowns that He has placed on our heads, and, touching our golden harps, we shall offer praise and thanksgiving to Him that sitteth on the throne.—RH September 3, 1903 quoted in CS 349, 350.

FULL OF JOY.—Heaven is full of joy. It resounds with the praises of Him who made so wonderful a sacrifice for the redemption of the human race. Should not the church on earth be full of praise? Should not Christians publish throughout the world the joy of serving Christ? Those who in heaven join with the angelic choir in their anthem of praise must learn on earth the song of heaven, the keynote of which is thanksgiving.—7T 244.

Jesus will receive you, all polluted as you are, and will wash you in His blood, and cleanse you from all pollution, and make you fit for the society of heavenly angels, in a pure, harmonious heaven. There is no jar, no discord, there. All is health, happiness, and joy.—2T 81.

NO PAIN THERE.—Pain cannot exist in the atmosphere of heaven. There will be no more tears, no funeral trains, no badges of mourning. "There shall be no more death, neither sorrow, nor crying: . . . for the former things are passed away." "The inhabitant shall not say, I am sick: the people that dwell therein shall be forgiven their iniquity." Revelation 21:4; Isaiah 33:24.—GC 676.

HOLINESS REIGNS SUPREME.—In heaven God is all in all. There, holiness reigns supreme; there is nothing to mar the perfect harmony with God. If we are indeed journeying thither, the spirit of heaven will dwell in our hearts here. But if we find no pleasure now in the contemplation of heavenly things; if we have no interest in seeking the knowledge of God, no delight in beholding the character of Christ; if holiness has no attractions for us—then we may be sure that our hope of heaven is vain. Perfect conformity to the will of God is the high aim to be constantly before the Christian. He will love to talk of God, of Jesus, of the home of bliss and purity which Christ has prepared for them that love Him. The contemplation of these themes, when the soul feasts upon the blessed assurances of God, the apostle represents as tasting "the powers of the world to come."—*Bible Echo* September 1, 1889 quoted in ML 293.

PERFECT ORDER.—God is a God of order. Everything connected with heaven is in perfect order; subjection and thorough discipline mark the movements of the angelic host. Success can only attend order and harmonious action. God requires order and system in His work now no less than in the days of Israel. All who are working for Him are to labor intelligently, not in a careless, haphazard manner. He would have His work done with faith and exactness, that He may place the seal of His approval upon it.— PP 376.

FULL EQUALITY.—The selfish principles exercised on the earth are not the principles which will prevail in heaven. All men stand on an equality in heaven.—RH March 31, 1896 quoted in CS 133.

REST IS PROMISED.—God designs that all shall be workers. The toiling beast of burden answers the purpose of its creation better than does the indolent man. God is a constant worker. The angels are workers; they are ministers of God to the children of men. Those who look forward to a heaven of inactivity will be disappointed, for the economy of heaven provides no place for the gratification of indolence. But to the weary and heavy-laden rest is promised. It is the faithful servant who will be welcomed from his labors to the joy of his Lord. He will lay off his armor with rejoicing, and will forget the noise of battle in the glorious rest prepared for those who conquer through the cross of Calvary.—CT 280.

SPIRIT OF UNSELFISH LOVE REIGNS.—In his sinless state, man held joyful communion with Him "in whom are hid all the treasures of wisdom and knowledge." Colossians 2:3. But after his sin, he could no longer find joy in holiness, and he sought to hide from the presence of God. Such is still the condition of the unrenewed heart. It is not in harmony with God, and finds no joy in communion with Him.

The sinner could not be happy in God's presence; he would shrink from the companionship of holy beings. Could he be permitted to enter heaven, it would have no joy for him. The spirit of unselfish love that reigns there— every heart responding to the heart of Infinite Love—would touch no answering chord in his soul. His thoughts, his interests, his motives, would be alien to those that actuate the sinless dwellers there. He would be a discordant note in the melody of heaven. Heaven would be to him a place of torture; he would long to be hidden from Him who is its light, and the center of its joy.

It is no arbitrary decree on the part of God that excludes the wicked from heaven; they are shut out by their own unfitness for its companionship. The glory of God would be to them a consuming fire. They would welcome destruction, that they might be hidden from the face of Him who died to redeem them.—SC 17, 18.

SOCIAL LIFE.—There we shall know even as also we are known. There the loves and sympathies that God has planted in the soul will find truest and sweetest exercise. The pure communion with holy beings, the harmonious social life with the blessed angels and with the faithful ones of all ages, the sacred fellowship that binds together "the whole family in heaven and earth"—all are among the experiences of the hereafter.—Ed 306 quoted in AH 548, 549.

CHAPTER

8

Face-to-Face
at Last

A NEW VIEW OF HEAVEN.—What a source of joy
to the disciples to know that they had such a Friend in
heaven to plead in their behalf! Through the visible ascension of Christ all their views and contemplation of
heaven are changed. Their minds had formerly dwelt
upon it as a region of unlimited space, tenanted by spirits without substance. Now heaven was connected with
the thought of Jesus, whom they had loved and rever-
enced above all others, with whom they had conversed
and journeyed, whom they had handled, even in His
resurrected body, who had spoken hope and comfort to
their hearts, and who, while the words were upon His
lips, had been taken up before their eyes, the tones of
His voice coming back to them as the cloudy chariot of
angels received Him: "Lo, I am with you alway, even
unto the end of the world."

Heaven could no longer appear to them as an indefinite, incomprehensible space, filled with intangible spirits. They now looked upon it as their future home, where mansions were being prepared for them by their loving Redeemer. Prayer was clothed with a new interest, since it was a communion with their Saviour. With new and thrilling emotions and a firm confidence that their prayer would be answered, they gathered in the upper chamber to offer their petitions and to claim the promise of the Saviour, who had said, "Ask, and ye shall receive, that your joy may be full." They prayed in the name of Jesus.

They had a gospel to preach—Christ in human form, a man of sorrows; Christ in humiliation, taken by wicked hands and crucified; Christ resurrected, and ascended to heaven, into the presence of God, to be man's Advocate; Christ to come again with power and great glory in the clouds of heaven.—3SP 262, 263 quoted in 6BC 1054.

THIS *SAME* JESUS.—Christ had ascended to heaven in the form of humanity. The disciples had beheld the cloud receive Him. The same Jesus who had walked and talked and prayed with them; who had broken bread with them; who had been with them in their boats on the lake; and who had that very day toiled with them up the ascent of Olivet—the same Jesus had now gone to share His Father's throne. And the angels had assured them that the very One whom they had seen go up into heaven, would come again even as He had ascended. He will come "with clouds; and every eye shall see Him."

"The Lord Himself shall descend from heaven with a

shout, with the voice of the Archangel, and with the trump of God: and the dead in Christ shall rise." "The Son of man shall come in His glory, and all the holy angels with Him, then shall He sit upon the throne of His glory." Revelation 1:7; 1 Thessalonians 4:16; Matthew 25:31. Thus will be fulfilled the Lord's own promise to His disciples: "If I go and prepare a place for you, I will come again, and receive you unto Myself; that where I am, there ye may be also." John 14:3. Well might the disciples rejoice in the hope of their Lord's return.—DA 832.

The disciples were still looking earnestly toward heaven when, "behold, two men stood by them in white apparel; which also said, Ye men of Galilee, why stand ye gazing up into heaven? this same Jesus, which is taken up from you into heaven, shall so come in like manner as ye have seen Him go into heaven." Acts 1:10, 11.

The promise of Christ's second coming was ever to be kept fresh in the minds of His disciples. The same Jesus whom they had seen ascending into heaven, would come again, to take to Himself those who here below give themselves to His service. The same voice that had said to them, "Lo, I am with you alway, even unto the end," would bid them welcome to His presence in the heavenly kingdom.—AA 33.

We Shall See Him as He Is.—When the children of God shall have put on immortality, they will "see Him as He is." 1 John 3:2. They will stand before the throne, accepted in the Beloved. All their sins have been blotted out, all their transgressions borne away. Now they can look upon the undimmed glory of the throne of God. They have been partakers with Christ in His sufferings, they have been workers together with Him in the plan of redemption, and they are partakers with Him in the joy of seeing souls saved in the kingdom of God, there to praise God through all eternity.—9T 285.

"If any man's work abide . . . he shall receive a reward." Glorious will be the reward bestowed when the faithful workers are gathered about the throne of God and the Lamb. When John in his mortal state beheld the glory of God, he fell as one dead; he was not able to endure the sight. But when mortal shall have put on immortality, the ransomed ones are like Jesus, for they see Him as He is. They stand before the throne, signifying that they are accepted. All their sins are blotted out, all their transgressions borne away. Now they can look upon the undimmed glory from the throne of God. They have been partakers with Christ of His sufferings, they have been workers together with Him in the plan of redemption, and they are partakers with Him in the joy of beholding souls saved through their instrumentality to praise God through all eternity.—5T 467.

HEAVEN'S KING.—When Christ came to this earth the first time, He came in lowliness and obscurity, and His life here was one of suffering and poverty. . . . At His second coming all will be changed. Not as a prisoner surrounded by a rabble will men see Him, but as heaven's King. Christ will come in His own glory, in the glory of His Father, and in the glory of the holy angels. Ten thousand times ten thousand and thousands of thousands of angels, the beautiful, triumphant sons of God, possessing surpassing loveliness and glory, will escort Him on His way. In the place of a crown of thorns, He will wear a crown of glory—a crown within a crown. In the place of that old purple robe, He will be clothed in a garment of whitest white, "so as no fuller on earth can white" (Mark 9:3) it. And on His vesture and on His thigh a name will be written, "King of kings, and Lord of lords."—RH November 13, 1913 quoted in AG 358.

RECEIVED IN HIS JOY.—The very One who gave His precious life for them, who by His grace moved their hearts to repentance, who awakened them to their need of repentance, receives them now into His joy. Oh, how they love Him! The realization of their hope is infinitely greater than their expectation. Their joy is complete, and they take their glittering crowns and cast them at their Redeemer's feet.— RH June 18, 1901 quoted in CS 349.

DESTINY FIXED AT SECOND COMING.—No literal devil, and probation after the coming of Christ, are fast becoming popular fables. The Scriptures plainly declare that every person's destiny is forever fixed at the coming of the Lord. Revelation 22:11, 12: "He that is unjust, let him be unjust still: and he which is filthy, let him be filthy still: and he that is righteous, let him be righteous still: and he that is holy, let him be holy still. And, behold, I come quickly; and My reward is with Me, to give every man according as his work shall be."—1T 342, 343.

A TIE NEVER TO BE BROKEN.—By His life and His death, Christ has achieved even more than recovery from the ruin wrought through sin. It was Satan's purpose to bring about an eternal separation between God and man; but in Christ we become more closely united to God than if we had never fallen. In taking our nature, the Saviour has bound Himself to humanity by a tie that is never to be broken. Through the eternal ages He is linked with us. "God so loved the world, that He gave His only begotten Son." John 3:16. He gave Him not only to bear our sins, and to die as our sacrifice; He gave Him to the fallen race. To assure us of His immutable counsel of peace, God gave His only-begotten Son to become one of the human family, forever to retain His human nature. This is the pledge that God will fulfill His word. "Unto us a child is born, unto us a son is given: and the government shall be upon His shoulder."

God has adopted human nature in the person of His Son, and has carried the same into the highest heaven. It is the "Son of man" who shares the throne of the universe. It is the "Son of man" whose name shall be called, "Wonderful, Counselor, The mighty God, The everlasting Father, The Prince of Peace." Isaiah 9:6. The I AM is the Daysman between God and humanity, laying His hand upon both. He who is "holy, harmless, undefiled, separate from sinners," is not ashamed to call us brethren. Hebrews 7:26; 2:11. In Christ the family of earth and the family of heaven are bound together. Christ glorified is our brother. Heaven is enshrined in humanity, and humanity is enfolded in the bosom of Infinite Love.—DA 25, 26.

ONE WITH THE RACE HE HAS REDEEMED.—"God so loved the world, that He gave His only begotten Son." He gave Him not only to live among men, to bear their sins, and die their sacrifice. He gave Him to the fallen race. Christ was to identify Himself with the interests and needs of humanity. He who was one with God has linked Himself with the children of men by ties that are never to be broken. Jesus is "not ashamed to call them brethren" (Hebrews 2:11); He is our Sacrifice, our Advocate, our Brother, bearing our human form before the Father's throne, and through eternal ages one with the race He has redeemed—the Son of man. And all this that man might be uplifted from the ruin and degradation of sin that he might reflect the love of God and share the joy of holiness.—SC 14.

RANSOMED HOST CHRIST'S CHIEF GLORY.—In the intercessory prayer of Jesus with His Father, He claimed that He had fulfilled the conditions which made it obligatory upon the Father to fulfill His part of the contract made in heaven, with regard to fallen man. . . . He declares Himself glorified in those who believe on Him. The church, in His name, is to carry to glorious perfection the work which He has commenced; and when that church shall be finally ransomed in the Paradise of God, He will look upon the travail of His soul and be satisfied. Through all eternity the ransomed host will be His chief glory.—3SP 260, 261 quoted in SD 296.

WILL BEAR HUMANITY THROUGHOUT ETERNITY.—Christ ascended to heaven, bearing a sanctified, holy humanity. He took this humanity with Him into the heavenly courts, and through the eternal ages He will bear it, as the One who has redeemed every human being in the city of God, the One who has pleaded before the Father, "I have graven them upon the palms of my hands." The palms of His hands bear the marks of the wounds that He received. If we are wounded and bruised, if we meet with difficulties that are hard to manage, let us remember how much Christ suffered for us. Let us sit together with our brethren in heavenly places in Christ. Let us bring heaven's blessing into our hearts.

Jesus took the nature of humanity, in order to reveal to man a pure, unselfish love, to teach us how to love one another.

As a man Christ ascended to heaven. As a man He is the substitute and surety for humanity. As a man He liveth to make intercession for us. He is preparing a place for all who love Him. As a man He will come again with power and glory, to receive His children. And that which should cause us joy and thanksgiving is, that God "hath appointed a day, in the which he will judge the world in righteousness by that man whom he hath ordained." Then we may have the assurance forever that the whole unfallen universe is interested in the grand work Jesus came to our world to accomplish, even the salvation of man.—Ms 16, 1890 quoted in 5BC 1125, 1126.

Christ has carried His humanity into eternity. He stands before God as the representative of our race. When we are clothed with the wedding garment of His righteousness, we become one with Him, and He says of us, "They shall walk with me in white: for they are worthy." His saints will behold Him in His glory, with no dimming veil between.— YI October 28, 1897 quoted in 7BC 925.

Christ ascended to heaven, bearing a sanctified, holy humanity. He took this humanity with Him into the heavenly courts, and through the eternal ages He will bear it, as the One who has redeemed every human being in the city of God.—RH March 9, 1905 quoted in 6BC 1054.

CHRIST'S HUMANITY PLEDGES GOD'S FAITHFULNESS.— We have everything we could ask to inspire us with faith and trust in God. In earthly courts, when a king would make his greatest pledge to assure men of his truth, he gives his child as a hostage, to be redeemed on the fulfillment of his promise; and behold what a pledge of the Father's faithfulness; for when He would assure men of the immutability of His council, He gave His only-begotten Son to come to earth, to take the nature of man, not only for the brief years of life, but to retain his nature in the heavenly courts, an everlasting pledge of the faithfulness of God. O the depth of the riches both of the wisdom and love of God! "Behold, what manner of love the Father hath bestowed upon us, that we should be called the sons of God" (1 John 3:1).— RH December 22, 1891 quoted in 1SM 258.

A MARVEL TO THE UNIVERSE.—This is the mystery of godliness. That Christ should take human nature, and by a life of humiliation elevate man in the scale of moral worth with God: that He should carry His adopted nature to the throne of God, and there present His children to the Father, to have conferred upon them an honor exceeding that conferred upon the angels—this is the marvel of the heavenly universe, the mystery into which angels desire to look. This is love that melts the sinner's heart.—Ms 21, 1900 quoted in SD 22.

9

Eden Restored

RESTORED MORE GLORIOUSLY.—The Garden of Eden remained upon the earth long after man had become an outcast from its pleasant paths. The fallen race were long permitted to gaze upon the home of innocence, their entrance barred only by the watching angels. At the cherubim-guarded gate of Paradise the divine glory was revealed. Hither came Adam and his sons to worship God. Here they renewed their vows of obedience to that law the transgression of which had banished them from Eden. When the tide of iniquity overspread the world, and the wickedness of men determined their destruction by a flood of waters, the hand that had planted Eden withdrew it from the earth. But in the final restitution, when there shall be "a new heaven and a new earth" (Revelation 21:1), it is to be restored more gloriously adorned than at the beginning.

Then they that have kept God's commandments shall breathe in immortal vigor beneath the tree of life; and through unending ages the inhabitants of sinless worlds shall behold, in that garden of delight, a sample of the perfect work of God's creation, untouched by the curse of sin— a sample of what the whole earth would have become, had man but fulfilled the Creator's glorious plan.—PP 62.

A Vision Given to Moses.—He saw the second coming of Christ in glory, the righteous dead raised to immortal life, and the living saints translated without seeing death, and together ascending with songs of gladness to the City of God.

Still another scene opens to his view—the earth freed from the curse, lovelier than the fair Land of Promise so lately spread out before him. There is no sin, and death cannot enter. There the nations of the saved find their eternal home. With joy unutterable Moses looks upon the scene—the fulfillment of a more glorious deliverance than his brightest hopes have ever pictured. Their earthly wanderings forever past, the Israel of God have at last entered the goodly land.—PP 477.

Eden Shall Bloom Again.—When Eden shall bloom on earth again, God's law of love will be obeyed by all beneath the sun.—MB 51.

The Earth Redeemed.—The great plan of redemption results in fully bringing back the world into God's favor. All that was lost by sin is restored. Not only man but the earth is redeemed, to be the eternal abode of the obedient. For six thousand years Satan has struggled to maintain possession of the earth. Now God's original purpose in its creation is accomplished. "The saints of the Most High shall take the kingdom, and possess the kingdom forever, even forever and ever." Daniel 7:18.

"From the rising of the sun unto the going down of the same the Lord's name is to be praised." Psalm 113:3. "In that day shall there be one Lord, and His name one." "And Jehovah shall be king over all the earth." Zechariah 14:9. Says the Scripture, "Forever, O Lord, Thy word is settled in heaven." "All His commandments are sure. They stand fast forever and ever." Psalms 119:89; 111:7, 8. The sacred statutes which Satan has hated and sought to destroy, will be honored throughout a sinless universe. And "as the earth bringeth forth her bud, and as the garden causeth the things that are sown in it to spring forth; so the Lord God will cause righteousness and praise to spring forth before all nations." Isaiah 61:11.—PP 342.

WHEN ADAM SEES EDEN AGAIN.—When the faithful dead shall be resurrected, and the king of glory shall open before them the gates of the city of God, and the nations who have kept the truth enter in, what beauty and glory will meet the astonished sight of those who have seen no greater beauties in the earth than that which they beheld in decaying nature after the threefold curse was upon the earth.

It is impossible to describe Adam's transports of joy as he again beholds Paradise, the Garden of Eden, his once happy home, from which, because of his transgression, he had been so long separated. He beholds the lovely flowers and trees, of every description for fruit and beauty, every one of which to designate them he had named while in his innocence. He sees the luxuriant vines, which had once been his delight to train upon bowers and trees.

But when he again beholds the widespread tree of life with its extended branches and glowing fruit, and to him again is granted access to its fruit and leaves, his gratitude is boundless. He first in adoration bows at the feet of the King of glory, and then with the redeemed host swells the song, Worthy, worthy is the Lamb that was slain. Adam had lost Eden by disobeying the commandments of God. He has now regained that lovely garden by repentance and faithful obedience. The curse rested upon him for disobedience, the blessing now for his obedience.—3SG 88, 89.

10

Who Will Be There?

CHRIST'S TROPHIES.—In that day the redeemed will shine forth in the glory of the Father and the Son. The angels, touching their golden harps, will welcome the King and His trophies of victory—those who have been washed and made white in the blood of the Lamb. A song of triumph will peal forth, filling all heaven. Christ has conquered. He enters the heavenly courts, accompanied by His redeemed ones, the witnesses that His mission of suffering and sacrifice has not been in vain. . . .

Jesus ascended to the Father as a representative of the human race, and God will bring those who reflect His image to behold and share with Him His glory.—9T 285, 286.

THOSE WHO SHARE CHRIST'S SUFFERING.—Those who are partakers of Christ's sufferings will also be partakers of His consolation and at last sharers of His glory.—AA 261.

GOD'S SURPRISES.—Many will be in heaven who their neighbors supposed would never enter there.—COL 72.

HEAVENLY COMPANIONS.—Then the redeemed will be welcomed to the home that Jesus is preparing for them. There their companions will not be the vile of earth, liars, idolaters, the impure, and unbelieving; but they will associate with those who have overcome Satan and through divine grace have formed perfect characters. Every sinful tendency, every imperfection, that afflicts them here has been removed by the blood of Christ, and the excellence and brightness of His glory, far exceeding the brightness of the sun, is imparted to them. And the moral beauty, the perfection of His character, shines through them, in worth far exceeding this outward splendor. They are without fault before the great white throne, sharing the dignity and the privileges of the angels.—SC 126.

BROTHERS CHARLES FITCH AND LEVI STOCKMAN.*—We all went under the tree [of life], and sat down to look at the glory of the place, when Brethren Fitch and Stockman, who had preached the gospel of the kingdom, and whom God had laid in the grave to save them, came up to us and asked us what we had passed through while they were sleeping. We tried to call up our greatest trials, but they looked so small compared with the far more exceeding and eternal weight of glory that surrounded us, that we could not speak

---

*Two Millerite Adventist ministers who died shortly before October 22, 1844.

them out, and we all cried out, "Alleluia! heaven is cheap enough!" and we touched our glorious harps and made heaven's arches ring.—LS 67.

HUGE MULTITUDE REDEEMED.—Nearest the throne are those who were once zealous in the cause of Satan, but who, plucked as brands from the burning, have followed their Saviour with deep, intense devotion. Next are those who perfected Christian characters in the midst of falsehood and infidelity, those who honored the law of God when the Christian world declared it void, and the millions, of all ages, who were martyred for their faith. And beyond is the "great multitude, which no man could number, of all nations, and kindreds, and people, and tongues . . . before the throne, and before the Lamb, clothed with white robes, and palms in their hands." Revelation 7:9. Their warfare is ended, their victory won. They have run the race and reached the prize. The palm branch in their hands is a symbol of their triumph, the white robe an emblem of the spotless righteousness of Christ which now is theirs.—GC 665.

CHRIST'S APOSTLES.—Amid the ransomed throng are the apostles of Christ, the heroic Paul, the ardent Peter, the loved and loving John, and their truehearted brethren, and with them the vast host of martyrs.—SR 424.

MARTYRS BURIED IN ROME.—In these underground retreats [the catacombs in Rome] the followers of Christ buried their dead; and here also, when suspected and proscribed, they found a home. When the Life-giver shall awaken those who have fought the good fight, many a martyr for Christ's sake will come forth from those gloomy caverns.—GC 40.

HIS FAITHFUL ONES.—With unutterable love, Jesus welcomes His faithful ones to the joy of their Lord. The Saviour's joy is in seeing, in the kingdom of glory, the souls that have been saved by His agony and humiliation. And the redeemed will be sharers in His joy, as they behold, among the blessed, those who have been won to Christ through their prayers, their labors, and their loving sacrifice. As they gather about the great white throne, gladness unspeakable will fill their hearts, when they behold those whom they have won for Christ, and see that one has gained others, and these still others, all brought into the haven of rest, there to lay their crowns at Jesus' feet and praise Him through the endless cycles of eternity.—GC 647.

ANGELS, SAINTS, AND SAVIOUR.—The angels will be there, also the resurrected saints with the martyrs, and the best of all, and what will cause us the most joy, our lovely Saviour, who suffered and died that we might enjoy that happiness and freedom, will be there. His glorious face will shine brighter than the sun, and light up the beautiful city and reflect glory all around.—YI October 1852 quoted in ML 357.

CHILDREN.—Children will be there. They will never be engaged in strife or discord. Their love will be fervent and holy. They will also have a crown of gold upon their heads and a harp in their hands. And their little countenances, that we here see so often troubled and perplexed, will beam with holy joy, expressive of their perfect freedom and happiness.—YI October 1852 quoted in ML 357.

A CONSOLATION LETTER.—Dear Brother: I hardly know what to say to you. The news of your wife's death was to me overwhelming. I could hardly believe it and can hardly believe it now. God gave me a view last Sabbath night which I will write. . . .

I saw that she was sealed and would come up at the voice of God and stand upon the earth, and would be with the 144,000. I saw we need not mourn for her; she would rest in the time of trouble, and all that we could mourn for was our loss in being deprived of her company. I saw her death would result in good.—Letter 10, 1850 quoted in 2SM 263.

THOSE WHO COME TO GOD IN FAITH.—God justly condemns all who do not make Christ their personal Saviour; but He pardons every soul who comes to Him in faith, and enables him to work the works of God, and through faith to be one with Christ. Jesus says of these, "I in them, and thou in me, that they may be made perfect in one [this unity brings perfection of character]; and that the world may know that thou hast sent me, and hast loved them, as thou hast loved me" (John 17:23).

The Lord has made every provision whereby man may have full and free salvation, and be complete in

Him. God designs that His children shall have the bright beams of the Sun of Righteousness, that all may have the light of truth. God has provided salvation for the world at infinite cost, even through the gift of His only-begotten Son. The apostle asks, "He that spared not his own Son, but delivered him up for us all, how shall he not with him also freely give us all things?" (Romans 8:32). Then if we are not saved, the fault will not be on the part of God, but on our part, that we have failed to cooperate with the divine agencies. Our will has not co-incided with God's will.—RH November 1, 1892 quoted in 1SM 375.

THOSE WHO LOOK TO JESUS.—He who is trying to reach heaven by his own works in keeping the law, is attempting an impossibility. Man cannot be saved without obedience, but his works should not be of himself; Christ should work in him to will and to do of His good pleasure. If a man could save himself by his own works, he might have something in himself in which to rejoice. The effort that man makes in his own strength to obtain salvation, is represented by the offering of Cain. All that man can do without Christ is polluted with selfishness and sin; but that which is wrought through faith is acceptable to God. When we seek to gain heaven through the merits of Christ, the soul makes progress. Looking unto Jesus, the author and finisher of our faith, we may go on from strength to strength, from victory to victory; for through Christ the grace of God has worked out our complete salvation.

Without faith it is impossible to please God. Living faith enables its possessor to lay hold on the merits of Christ, enables him to derive great comfort and satisfaction from the plan of salvation.—RH July 1, 1890 quoted in 1SM 364.

THOSE WHO CLING TO JESUS.—Our Saviour is the ladder which Jacob saw, whose base rested on the earth and whose topmost rounds reached the highest heavens. This shows the appointed method of salvation. If any of us are finally saved, it will be by clinging to Jesus as to the rounds of a ladder.—5T 539.

ELECT OBEY WITH CHILDLIKE SIMPLICITY.—The Father sets His love upon His elect people who live in the midst of men. These are the people whom Christ has redeemed by the price of His own blood; and because they respond to the drawing of Christ, through the sovereign mercy of God, they are elected to be saved as His obedient children. Upon them is manifested the free grace of God, the love wherewith He hath loved them. Everyone who will humble himself as a little child, who will receive and obey the word of God with a child's simplicity, will be among the elect of God.—ST January 2, 1893 quoted in OHC 77.

THE 144,000.—We were on our way to Mount Zion. As we were traveling along, we met a company who were also gazing at the glories of the place. I noticed red as a border on their garments; their crowns were brilliant; their robes were pure white. As we greeted them, I asked Jesus who they were. He said they were martyrs that had been slain for Him. With them was an innumerable company of little ones; they had a hem of red on their garments also. Mount Zion was just before us, and on the mount was a glorious temple, and about it were seven other mountains, on which grew roses and lilies. And I saw the little ones climb, or, if they chose, use their little wings and fly to the top of the mountains, and pluck the never-fading flowers.

There were all kinds of trees around the temple to beautify the place—the box, the pine, the fir, the oil, the myrtle, the pomegranate, and the fig tree bowed down with the weight of its timely figs; these made the place all over glorious. And as we were about to enter the temple, Jesus raised His lovely voice and said, "Only the 144,000 enter this place," and we shouted, "Alleluia!"

This temple was supported by seven pillars, all of transparent gold, set with pearls most glorious. The wonderful things I there saw, I cannot describe. Oh, that I could talk in the language of Canaan, then could I tell a little of the glory of the better world. I saw there tables of stone in which the names of the 144,000 were engraved in letters of gold.—1T 68, 69.

God's Promise to Ellen White.—The Lord has given me a view of other worlds. Wings were given me, and an angel attended me from the city to a place that was bright and glorious. . . . I begged of my attending angel to let me remain in that place. I could not bear the thought of coming back to this dark world again. Then the angel said, "You must go back, and if you are faithful, you, with the

144,000, shall have the privilege of visiting all the worlds and viewing the handiwork of God."—EW 39, 40.

ABEL WILL RECEIVE IMMORTALITY.—At His second coming all the precious dead, from righteous Abel to the last saint that dies, shall awake to glorious, immortal life.—ST April 22, 1913 quoted in 5BC 1110.

ABRAHAM'S ETERNAL POSSESSION.—The plan of redemption was here opened to him, in the death of Christ, the great sacrifice, and His coming in glory. Abraham saw also the earth restored to its Eden beauty, to be given him for an everlasting possession, as the final and complete fulfillment of the promise.—PP 137.

OVERCOMERS WILL RECEIVE CROWN.—Let no man flatter himself that he is a successful man unless he preserves the integrity of his conscience, giving himself wholly to the truth and to God. We should move steadily forward, never losing heart or hope in the good work, whatever trials beset our path, whatever moral darkness may encompass us. Patience, faith, and love for duty are the lessons we must learn. Subduing self and looking to Jesus is an everyday work. The Lord will never forsake the soul that trusts in Him and seeks His aid. The crown of life is placed only upon the brow of the overcomer. There is, for everyone, earnest, solemn work for God while life lasts. As Satan's power increases and his devices are multiplied, skill, aptness, and sharp generalship should be exercised by those in charge of the flock of God. Not only have we each a work to do for our own souls, but we have also a duty to arouse others to gain eternal life.—5T 70, 71.

If you would be a saint in heaven you must first be a saint on earth. The traits of character you cherish in life will not be changed by death or by the resurrection. You will come up from the grave with the same disposition you manifested in your home and in society. Jesus does not change the character at His coming. The work of transformation must be done now. Our daily lives are determining our destiny. Defects of character must be repented of and overcome through the grace of Christ, and a symmetrical character must be formed while in this probationary state, that we may be fitted for the mansions above.—Letter 18b, 1891 quoted in LDE 295.

God's original purpose in the creation of the earth is fulfilled as it is made the eternal abode of the redeemed. "The righteous shall inherit the land, and dwell therein forever."

Then we shall enjoy with Him all the glories of the world to come throughout the ceaseless ages of eternity. . . . There is nothing in the kingdom of God to disturb or annoy. This is the life that is promised to the overcomer—a life of happiness and peace, a life of love and beauty. . . . There is no sin, no distracting care, nothing to mar the peace of the inhabitant.—ML 350.

Those that overcome the world, the flesh, and the devil, will be the favored ones who shall receive the seal of the living God. Those whose hands are not clean, whose hearts are not pure, will not have the seal of the living God. Those who are planning sin and acting it will be passed by. Only those who, in their attitude before God, are filling the position of those who are repenting and confessing their sins in the great anti-typical day of atonement, will be recognized and marked as worthy of God's protection. The names of those who are steadfastly looking and waiting and watching for the appearing of their Saviour—more earnestly and wishfully than they who wait for the morning—will be numbered with those who are sealed.

Those who, while having all the light of truth flashing upon their souls, should have works corresponding to their avowed faith, but are allured by sin, setting up idols in their hearts, corrupting their souls before God, and polluting those who unite with them in sin, will have their names blotted out of the book of life, and be left in midnight darkness, having no oil in their vessels with their lamps. "Unto you that fear My name shall the Sun of Righteousness arise with healing in His wings."—TM 445.

There is a heaven before us, a crown of life to win. But to the overcomer only is the reward given. He who gains heaven must be clothed with the robe of righteousness. "Every man that hath this hope in him purifieth himself, even as he is pure." In the character of Christ there was no discord of any kind. And this must be our experience. Our lives must be controlled by the principles that controlled His life.—Ms 28, 1886 quoted in SD 8.

FAITHFUL, EXALTED, AND HONORED.—The glories that await the faithful overcomer are beyond any description. The Lord will greatly honor and exalt His faithful ones. They shall grow like the cedar, and their comprehension will be certainly increasing. And at every advanced stage of knowledge their anticipation will fall far beneath the reality. "Eye hath not seen, nor ear heard, neither have entered into the heart of man, the things which God hath prepared for them that love him" (1 Corinthians 2:9). Our work now is to prepare for those mansions that God is preparing for those who love Him and keep His commandments. . . . The Lord Jesus will enlarge every mind and heart for the reception of the Holy Spirit.—Letter 71, 1900 quoted in UL 151.

THOSE WHO HAVE COME BACK TO THE FOLD.—When the storm of persecution really breaks upon us, the true sheep will hear the true Shepherd's voice. Self-denying efforts will be put forth to save the lost, and many who have strayed from the fold will come back to follow the great Shepherd.—Australian *Signs of the Times, Supplement,* January 26, 1903 quoted in ChS 166.

HIS WELL-BELOVED BROTHERS.—The black man's name is written in the book of life beside the white man's. All are one in Christ. Birth, station, nationality, or color cannot elevate or degrade men. The character makes the man. If a red man, a Chinaman, or an African gives his heart to God in obedience and faith, Jesus loves him none the less for his color. He calls him His well-beloved brother.—*The Southern Work,* p. 8 quoted in ChS 218.

Those the Redeemed Have Taught About Jesus.—
The redeemed will meet and recognize those whose attention they have directed to the uplifted Saviour. What
blessed converse they have with these souls! "I was a sinner," it will be said, "without God and without hope in
the world, and you came to me and drew my attention to
the precious Saviour as my only hope." . . . Others will
say, "I was a heathen in heathen lands. You left your friends
and comfortable home and came to teach me how to find
Jesus and believe in Him as the only true God. I demol-
ished my idols and worshiped God, and now I see Him
face to face. I am saved, eternally saved, ever to behold
Him whom I love."—RH January 5, 1905 quoted in ML
353.

Soul Winners.—Every wise steward of the means en-
trusted to him, will enter into the joy of his Lord. What is
this joy?—"Likewise, I say unto you, there is joy in the
presence of the angels of God over one sinner that
repenteth." There will be a blessed commendation, a holy
benediction, on the faithful winners of souls. They will
join the rejoicing ones in heaven, who shout the harvest
home.—RH October 10, 1907 quoted in CS 348.

Those Who Have Heaven in Their Hearts.—To His
faithful followers Christ has been a daily companion and
familiar friend. They have lived in close contact, in constant
communion with God. Upon them the glory of the Lord
has risen. In them the light of the knowledge of the glory of
God in the face of Jesus Christ has been reflected. Now they

rejoice in the undimmed rays of the brightness and glory of the King in His majesty. They are prepared for the communion of heaven; for they have heaven in their hearts.

With uplifted heads, with the bright beams of the Sun of Righteousness shining upon them, with rejoicing that their redemption draweth nigh, they go forth to meet the Bridegroom, saying, "Lo, this is our God; we have waited for Him, and He will save us." Isaiah 25:9.

"And I heard as it were the voice of a great multitude, and as the voice of many waters, and as the voice of mighty thunderings, saying, Alleluia; for the Lord God omnipotent reigneth. Let us be glad and rejoice, and give honour to Him; for the marriage of the Lamb is come, and His wife hath made herself ready. . . . And he saith unto me, Write, Blessed are they which are called unto the marriage supper of the Lamb." "He is Lord of lords, and King of kings; and they that are with Him are called, and chosen, and faithful." Revelation 19:6-9; 17:14.—COL 421.

ABRAHAM, ISAAC, JACOB, NOAH, DANIEL.—In another passage from the book *A Word to the Little Flock,* I speak of scenes upon the new earth, and state that I there saw holy men of old, "Abraham, Isaac, Jacob, Noah, Daniel and many like them."—Ms 4, 1883 quoted in 1SM 64.

THOSE WHO HAVE FOLLOWED THE PATTERN.—The waiting saints will be looking for Him, and gazing into heaven, as were the "men of Galilee" when He ascended from the Mount of Olivet. Then, those only who are holy, those who have followed fully the meek Pattern will, with rapturous joy, exclaim as they behold Him, "Lo, this is our God; we have waited for him, and he will save us." And they will be changed "in a moment, in the twinkling of an eye, at the last trump," that wakes the sleeping saints, and calls them forth from their dusty beds, clothed with glorious immortality, shouting Victory! Victory! over death and the grave. The changed saints are caught up together with them to meet the Lord in the air, never more to be separated from the object of their love.—RH June 10, 1852 quoted in SD 360.

THOSE WHO DO HIS WILL.—The character which we now manifest is deciding our future destiny. The happiness of heaven will be found by conforming to the will of God, and if men become members of the royal family in heaven, it will be because heaven has begun with them on earth. . . . The righteous will take every grace, every precious, sanctified ability, into the courts above, and exchange earth for heaven. God knows who are the loyal and true subjects of His kingdom on earth, and those who do His will upon earth as it is done in heaven, will be made the members of the royal family above.—RH March 26, 1895 quoted in SD 361.

THOSE WHO WORK IN HARMONY WITH GOD.—No one, not even God, can carry us to heaven unless we make the necessary effort on our part. We must put features of beauty into our lives. We must expel the unlovely natural traits that make us unlike Jesus. While God works in us to will and to do of His own good pleasure, we must work in harmony with Him. The religion of Christ transforms the heart. It makes the worldly-minded man heavenly-minded. Under its influence the selfish man becomes unselfish because this is the character of Christ. The dishonest, scheming man becomes upright, so that it is second nature to him to do unto others as he would have others do unto him. The profligate is changed from impurity to purity. He forms correct habits, for the gospel of Christ has become to him a savor of life unto life.—5T 345.

THOSE WHO CONTEMPLATE HEAVENLY THINGS.—In heaven God is all in all. There holiness reigns supreme; there is nothing to mar the perfect harmony with God. If we are indeed journeying thither, the spirit of heaven will dwell in our hearts here. But if we find no pleasure now in the contemplation of heavenly things; if we have no interest in seeking the knowledge of God, no delight in beholding the character of Christ; if holiness has no attractions for us—then we may be sure that our hope of heaven is vain. Perfect conformity to the will of God is the high aim to be constantly before the Christian. He will love to talk of God, of Jesus, of the home of bliss and purity which Christ has prepared for them that love Him. The contemplation of these themes, when the soul feasts upon the blessed assurances of God, the apostle represents as tasting the powers of the world to come.—5T 745.

THOSE WHO LOVE GOD AND NEIGHBORS.—"Thou shalt love the Lord thy God with all thy heart, and with all thy soul, and with all thy strength, and with all thy mind; and thy neighbour as thyself. . . . This do, and thou shalt live"

(Luke 10:27, 28). All who will conform their lives to the plain requirements of God's Word will inherit eternal life.— Ms 28, 1904 quoted in 1SM 174.

THOSE WHO HAVE PARTAKEN IN CHRIST'S SUFFERINGS.—Those only who have partaken of the sufferings of the Son of God, and have come up through great tribulation, and have washed their robes and made them white in the blood of the Lamb, can enjoy the indescribable glory and unsurpassed beauty of heaven.—1T 155.

THOSE CLOTHED WITH PURITY.—Soon Christ is coming for His people to take them to the mansions He is preparing for them. But nothing that defiles can enter those mansions. Heaven is pure and holy, and those who pass through the gates of the City of God must here be clothed with inward and outward purity.—RH June 10, 1902 quoted in CH 103.

THOSE WHO HAVE HEARD HIS VOICE.—Those whom Christ commends in the judgment may have known little of theology, but they have cherished His principles. Through the influence of the divine Spirit they have been a blessing to those about them. Even among the heathen are those who have cherished the spirit of kindness; before the words of life had fallen upon their ears, they have befriended the missionaries, even ministering to them at the peril of their own lives. Among the heathen are those who worship God ignorantly, those to whom the light is never brought by human instrumentality, yet they will not perish. Though ignorant of the written law of God, they have heard His voice speaking to them in nature, and have done the things that the law required. Their works are evidence that the Holy Spirit has touched their hearts, and they are recognized as the children of God.

How surprised and gladdened will be the lowly among the nations, and among the heathen, to hear from the lips of the Saviour, "Inasmuch as ye have done it unto one of the least of these My brethren, ye have done it unto Me"! How glad will be the heart of Infinite Love as His followers look up with surprise and joy at His words of approval!

But not to any class is Christ's love restricted. He identifies Himself with every child of humanity. That we might become members of the heavenly family, He became a member of the earthly family. He is the Son of man, and thus a brother to every son and daughter of Adam. His followers are not to feel themselves detached from the perishing world around them. They are a part of the great web of humanity; and Heaven looks upon them as brothers to sinners as well as to saints. The fallen, the erring, and the sinful, Christ's love embraces; and every deed of kindness done to uplift a fallen soul, every act of mercy, is accepted as done to Him.—DA 638.

11

Some Are Already in Heaven

ENOCH.—Enoch's heart was upon eternal treasures. He had looked upon the celestial city. He had seen the King in His glory in the midst of Zion. His mind, his heart, his conversation, were in heaven. The greater the existing iniquity, the more earnest was his longing for the home of God. While still on earth, he dwelt, by faith, in the realms of light.

"Blessed are the pure in heart: for they shall see God." Matthew 5:8. For three hundred years Enoch had been seeking purity of soul, that he might be in harmony with Heaven. For three centuries he had walked with God. Day by day he had longed for a closer union; nearer and nearer had grown the communion, until God took him to Himself. He had stood at the threshold of the eternal world, only a step between him and the land of the blest; and now the portals opened, the walk with God, so long pursued on earth, con-

tinued, and he passed through the gates of the Holy City—
the first from among men to enter there.—PP 87.

MOSES.—Christ Himself, with the angels who had buried Moses, came down from heaven to call forth the sleeping saint. Satan had exulted at his success in causing Moses
to sin against God, and thus come under the dominion of
death. The great adversary declared that the divine sentence—"Dust thou art, and unto dust shalt thou return"
(Genesis 3:19)—gave him possession of the dead. The
power of the grave had never been broken, and all who
were in the tomb he claimed as his captives, never to be
released from his dark prison house.

For the first time Christ was about to give life to the
dead. As the Prince of life and the shining ones approached
the grave, Satan was alarmed for his supremacy. With his
evil angels he stood to dispute an invasion of the territory
that he claimed as his own. He boasted that the servant of
God had become his prisoner. He declared that even Moses
was not able to keep the law of God; that he had taken to
himself the glory due to Jehovah—the very sin which had
caused Satan's banishment from heaven—and by transgression had come under the dominion of Satan. The archtraitor
reiterated the original charges that he had made against
the divine government, and repeated his complaints of
God's injustice toward him.

Christ did not stoop to enter into controversy with Satan. He might have brought against him the cruel work
which his deceptions had wrought in heaven, causing the
ruin of a vast number of its inhabitants. He might have

pointed to the falsehoods told in Eden, that had led to Adam's sin and brought death upon the human race. He might have reminded Satan that it was his own work in tempting Israel to murmuring and rebellion, which had wearied the long-suffering patience of their leader, and in an unguarded moment had surprised him into the sin for which he had fallen under the power of death. But Christ referred all to His Father, saying, "The Lord rebuke thee." Jude 9.

The Saviour entered into no dispute with His adversary, but He then and there began His work of breaking the power of the fallen foe, and bringing the dead to life. Here was an evidence that Satan could not controvert, of the supremacy of the Son of God. The resurrection was forever made certain. Satan was despoiled of his prey; the righteous dead would live again.

In consequence of sin Moses had come under the power of Satan. In his own merits he was death's lawful captive; but he was raised to immortal life, holding his title in the name of the Redeemer. Moses came forth from the tomb glorified, and ascended with his Deliverer to the City of God.

Never, till exemplified in the sacrifice of Christ, were the justice and the love of God more strikingly displayed than in His dealings with Moses. God shut Moses out of Canaan, to teach a lesson which should never be forgotten—that He requires exact obedience, and that men are to beware of taking to themselves the glory which is due to their Maker. He could not grant the prayer of Moses that he might share the inheritance of Israel, but He did not forget or forsake His servant. The God of heaven understood the suffering that

Moses had endured; He had noted every act of faithful service through those long years of conflict and trial. On the top of Pisgah, God called Moses to an inheritance infinitely more glorious than the earthly Canaan.

Upon the mount of transfiguration Moses was present with Elijah, who had been translated. They were sent as bearers of light and glory from the Father to His Son. And thus the prayer of Moses, uttered so many centuries before, was at last fulfilled. He stood upon the "goodly mountain," within the heritage of his people, bearing witness to Him in whom all the promises to Israel centered. Such is the last scene revealed to mortal vision in the history of that man so highly honored of Heaven.—PP 478, 479.

ELIJAH.—"And it came to pass, as they still went on, and talked, that, behold, there appeared a chariot of fire, and horses of fire, and parted them both asunder; and Elijah went up by a whirlwind into heaven." See 2 Kings 2:1-11.

Elijah was a type of the saints who will be living on the earth at the time of the second advent of Christ and who will be "changed, in a moment, in the twinkling of an eye, at the last trump," without tasting of death. 1 Corinthians 15:51, 52. It was as a representative of those who shall be thus translated that Elijah, near the close of Christ's earthly ministry, was permitted to stand with Moses by the side of the Saviour on the mount of transfiguration. In these glorified ones, the disciples saw in miniature a representation of the kingdom of the redeemed. They beheld Jesus clothed with the light of heaven; they heard the "voice out of the cloud" (Luke 9:35), acknowledging Him as the Son of God;

they saw Moses, representing those who will be raised from the dead at the time of the second advent; and there also stood Elijah, representing those who at the close of earth's history will be changed from mortal to immortal and be translated to heaven without seeing death.

In the desert, in loneliness and discouragement, Elijah had said that he had had enough of life and had prayed that he might die. But the Lord in His mercy had not taken him at his word. There was yet a great work for Elijah to do; and when his work was done, he was not to perish in discouragement and solitude. Not for him the descent into the tomb, but the ascent with God's angels to the presence of His glory.—PK 227, 228.

Moses and Elijah.—Moses upon the mount of transfiguration was a witness to Christ's victory over sin and death. He represented those who shall come from the grave at the resurrection of the just. Elijah, who had been translated to heaven without seeing death, represented those who will be living upon the earth at Christ's second coming, and who will be "changed, in a moment, in the twinkling of an eye, at the last trump;" when "this mortal must put on immortality," and "this corruptible must put on incorruption." 1 Corinthians 15:51-53. Jesus was clothed with the light of heaven, as He will appear when He shall come "the second time without sin unto salvation." For He will come "in the glory of His Father with the holy angels." Hebrews 9:28; Mark 8:38.

The Saviour's promise to the disciples was now fulfilled. Upon the mount the future kingdom of glory was represented in miniature—Christ the King, Moses a representative of the risen saints, and Elijah of the translated ones.—DA 421, 422.

SPECIAL RESURRECTION.—Christ arose from the dead as the first fruits of those that slept. He was the antitype of the wave sheaf, and His resurrection took place on the very day when the wave sheaf was to be presented before the Lord. For more than a thousand years this symbolic ceremony had been performed. From the harvest fields the first heads of ripened grain were gathered, and when the people went up to Jerusalem to the Passover, the sheaf of first fruits was waved as a thank offering before the Lord. Not until this was presented could the sickle be put to the grain, and it be gathered into sheaves. The sheaf dedicated to God represented the harvest. So Christ the first fruits represented the great spiritual harvest to be gathered for the kingdom of God. His resurrection is the type and pledge of the resurrection of all the righteous dead. "For if we believe that Jesus died and rose again, even so them also which sleep in Jesus will God bring with Him." 1 Thessalonians 4:14.

As Christ arose, He brought from the grave a multitude of captives. The earthquake at His death had rent open their graves, and when He arose, they came forth with Him. They were those who had been co-laborers with God, and who at the cost of their lives had borne testimony to the truth. Now they were to be witnesses for Him who had raised them from the dead.

During His ministry, Jesus had raised the dead to life.

He had raised the son of the widow of Nain, and the ruler's daughter and Lazarus. But these were not clothed with immortality. After they were raised, they were still subject to death. But those who came forth from the grave at Christ's resurrection were raised to everlasting life. They ascended with Him as trophies of His victory over death and the grave. These, said Christ, are no longer the captives of Satan; I have redeemed them. I have brought them from the grave as the first fruits of My power, to be with Me where I am, nevermore to see death or experience sorrow.

These went into the city, and appeared unto many, declaring, Christ has risen from the dead, and we be risen with Him. Thus was immortalized the sacred truth of the resurrection. The risen saints bore witness to the truth of the words, "Thy dead men shall live, together with My dead body shall they arise." Their resurrection was an illustration of the fulfillment of the prophecy, "Awake and sing, ye that dwell in dust: for thy dew is as the dew of herbs, and the earth shall cast out the dead." Isaiah 26:19.

To the believer, Christ is the resurrection and the life. In our Saviour the life that was lost through sin is restored; for He has life in Himself.—DA 785, 786.

CHAPTER

12

Some Who Will Not Be There

CAIN— Notwithstanding that Cain had by his crimes merited the sentence of death, a merciful Creator still spared his life, and granted him opportunity for repentance. But Cain lived only to harden his heart, to encourage rebellion against the divine authority, and to become the head of a line of bold, abandoned sinners. This one apostate, led on by Satan, became a tempter to others; and his example and influence exerted their demoralizing power, until the earth became so corrupt and filled with violence as to call for its destruction.—PP 78.

LOT'S WIFE.—If Lot himself had manifested no hesitancy to obey the angels' warning, but had earnestly fled toward the mountains, without one word of pleading or remonstrance, his wife also would have made her escape. The influence of his example would have saved her from the sin that sealed her doom. But his hesitancy and delay caused her to lightly regard the divine warning. While her body was upon the plain, her heart clung to Sodom, and she perished with it. She rebelled against God because His judgments involved her possessions and her children in the ruin. Although so greatly favored in being called out from the wicked city, she felt that she was severely dealt with, because the wealth that it had taken years to accumulate must be left to destruction. Instead of thankfully accepting deliverance, she presumptuously looked back to desire the life of those who had rejected the divine warning. Her sin showed her to be unworthy of life, for the preservation of which she felt so little gratitude.—PP 161, 162.

KING SAUL.—Saul knew that in this last act, of consulting the witch of Endor, he cut the last shred which held him to God. He knew that if he had not before willfully separated himself from God, this act sealed that separation, and made it final. He had made an agreement with death, and a covenant with hell. The cup of his iniquity was full.—1SP 376, 377.

JUDAS.—God has appointed means, if we will use them diligently and prayerfully, that no vessel shall be shipwrecked, but outride the tempest and storm, and anchor in the haven of bliss at last. But if we despise and neglect these appointments and privileges, God will not work a miracle to save any of us, and we will be lost as were Judas and Satan.—TM 453.

HEROD, HERODIAS, PILATE, AND INDIVIDUALS DIRECTLY
INVOLVED IN JESUS' CRUCIFIXION.—And now before the
swaying multitude are revealed the final scenes—the patient Sufferer treading the path to Calvary; the Prince of
heaven hanging upon the cross; the haughty priests and
the jeering rabble deriding His expiring agony; the supernatural darkness; the heaving earth, the rent rocks, the open
graves, marking the moment when the world's Redeemer
yielded up His life.

The awful spectacle appears just as it was. Satan, his
angels, and his subjects have no power to turn from the
picture of their own work. Each actor recalls the part which
he performed. Herod, who slew the innocent children of
Bethlehem that he might destroy the King of Israel; the
base Herodias, upon whose guilty soul rests the blood of
John the Baptist; the weak, timeserving Pilate; the mocking soldiers; the priests and rulers and the maddened throng
who cried, "His blood be on us, and on our children!"—
all behold the enormity of their guilt. They vainly seek to
hide from the divine majesty of His countenance, outshin-
ing the glory of the sun, while the redeemed cast their
crowns at the Saviour's feet, exclaiming: "He died for me!"
—GC 667.

Those who derided His claim to be the Son of God
are speechless now. There is the haughty Herod who jeered
at His royal title and bade the mocking soldiers crown
Him king. There are the very men who with impious
hands placed upon His form the purple robe, upon His
sacred brow the thorny crown, and in His unresisting hand

the mimic scepter, and bowed before Him in blasphemous mockery. The men who smote and spit upon the Prince of life now turn from His piercing gaze and seek to flee from the overpowering glory of His presence. Those who drove the nails through His hands and feet, the soldier who pierced His side, behold these marks with terror and remorse.

With awful distinctness do priests and rulers recall the events of Calvary. With shuddering horror they remember how, wagging their heads in satanic exultation, they exclaimed: "He saved others; Himself He cannot save. If He be the King of Israel, let Him now come down from the cross, and we will believe Him. He trusted in God; let Him deliver Him now, if He will have Him." Matthew 27:42, 43.

Vividly they recall the Saviour's parable of the husbandmen who refused to render to their lord the fruit of the vineyard, who abused his servants and slew his son. They remember, too, the sentence which they themselves pronounced: The lord of the vineyard "will miserably destroy those wicked men." In the sin and punishment of those unfaithful men the priests and elders see their own course and their own just doom. And now there rises a cry of mortal agony. Louder than the shout, "Crucify Him, crucify Him," which rang through the streets of Jerusalem, swells the awful, despairing wail, "He is the Son of God! He is the true Messiah!" They seek to flee from the presence of the King of kings. In the deep caverns of the earth, rent asunder by the warring of the elements, they vainly attempt to hide.—GC 643, 644.

NERO AND HIS MOTHER; PAPAL PRIESTS AND PON-
TIFFS.—Amid the ransomed throng are the apostles of
Christ, the heroic Paul, the ardent Peter, the loved and
loving John, and their truehearted brethren, and with
them the vast host of martyrs; while outside the walls,
with every vile and abominable thing, are those by whom
they were persecuted, imprisoned, and slain. There is
Nero, that monster of cruelty and vice, beholding the joy
and exaltation of those whom he once tortured, and in
whose extremest anguish he found satanic delight. His
mother is there to witness the result of her own work; to
see how the evil stamp of character transmitted to her
son, the passions encouraged and developed by her influence and example, have borne fruit in crimes that caused
the world to shudder.

There are papist priests and prelates, who claimed to
be Christ's ambassadors, yet employed the rack, the dun-
geon, and the stake to control the consciences of His
people. There are the proud pontiffs who exalted themselves above God and presumed to change the law of the
Most High. Those pretended fathers of the church have
an account to render to God from which they would fain
be excused. Too late they are made to see that the Omni-
scient One is jealous of His law and that He will in no
wise clear the guilty. They learn now that Christ identifies His interest with that of His suffering people; and
they feel the force of His own words: "Inasmuch as ye
have done it unto one of the least of these My brethren,
ye have done it unto Me." Matthew 25:40.—GC 667,
668.

THE WICKED OF ALL GENERATIONS.—In fearful majesty He [Jesus] calls forth the wicked dead. They are wakened from their long sleep. What a dreadful waking! They behold the Son of God in His stern majesty and resplendent glory. All, as soon as they behold Him, know that He is the crucified one who died to save them, whom they had despised and rejected. They are in number like the sand upon the sea shore. At the first resurrection all come forth in immortal bloom, but at the second, the marks of the curse are visible upon all. All come up as they went down into their graves.

Those who lived before the flood, come forth with their giant-like stature, more than twice as tall as men now living upon the earth, and well proportioned. The generations after the flood were less in stature. There was a continual decrease through successive generations, down to the last that lived upon the earth. The contrast between the first wicked men who lived upon the earth, and those of the last generation, was very great. The first were of lofty height and well proportioned—the last came up as they went down, a dwarfed, feeble, deformed race.—3SG 84.

With fiendish exultation he [Satan] points to the unnumbered millions who have been raised from the dead and declares that as their leader he is well able to overthrow the city and regain his throne and his kingdom.

In that vast throng are multitudes of the long-lived race that existed before the Flood; men of lofty stature and giant intellect, who, yielding to the control of fallen angels, devoted all their skill and knowledge to the exaltation of themselves; men whose wonderful works of art led the world to idolize their genius, but whose cruelty and evil inventions, defiling the earth and defacing the image of God, caused Him to blot them from the face of His creation. There are kings and generals who conquered nations, valiant men who never lost a battle, proud, ambitious warriors whose approach made kingdoms tremble. In death these experienced no change. As they come up from the grave, they resume the current of their thoughts just where it ceased. They are actuated by the same desire to conquer that ruled them when they fell.—GC 663, 664.

THOSE LIVING A LIFE OF SELFISHNESS.—Let none suppose that they can live a life of selfishness, and then, having served their own interests, enter into the joy of their Lord. In the joy of unselfish love they could not participate. They would not be fitted for the heavenly courts. They could not appreciate the pure atmosphere of love that pervades heaven. The voices of the angels and the music of their harps would not satisfy them. To their minds the science of heaven would be as an enigma.—COL 364, 365.

THE SPIRITUALLY BENUMBED.—How little do the young suffer, or deny self, for their religion! To sacrifice is scarcely thought of among them. They entirely fail of imitating the Pattern in this respect. I saw that the language of their lives is: Self must be gratified, pride must be indulged. They forget the Man of Sorrows, who was acquainted with grief. The sufferings of Jesus in Gethsemane, His sweating as it were great drops of blood in the garden, the platted crown of thorns that pierced His holy brow, do not move them. They have become benumbed. Their sensibilities are blunted, and they have lost all sense of the great sacrifice made for them. They can sit and listen to the story of the cross, hear how the cruel nails were driven through the hands and feet of the Son of God, and it does not stir the depths of the soul.

Said the angel: "If such should be ushered into the city of God, and told that all its rich beauty and glory was theirs to enjoy eternally, they would have no sense of how dearly that inheritance was purchased for them. They would never realize the matchless depths of a Saviour's love. They have not drunk of the cup, nor been baptized with the baptism. Heaven would be marred if such should dwell there. Those only who have partaken of the sufferings of the Son of God, and have come up through great tribulation, and have washed their robes and made them white in the blood of the Lamb, can enjoy the indescribable glory and unsurpassed beauty of heaven."—1T 155.

I have seen an angel standing with scales in his hands weighing the thoughts and interest of the people of God, especially the young. In one scale were the thoughts and interest tending heavenward; in the other were the thoughts and interest tending to earth. And in this scale were thrown all the reading of storybooks, thoughts of dress and show, vanity, pride, etc. Oh, what a solemn moment! the angels of God standing with scales, weighing the thoughts of His professed children—those who claim to be dead to the world and alive to God. The scale filled with thoughts of

earth, vanity, and pride quickly went down, notwithstanding weight after weight rolled from the scale. The one with
the thoughts and interest tending to heaven went quickly
up as the other went down, and oh, how light it was! I can
relate this as I saw it; but never can I give the solemn and
vivid impression stamped upon my mind, as I saw the angel with the scales weighing the thoughts and interest of
the people of God. Said the angel: "Can such enter heaven?
No, no, never. Tell them the hope they now possess is vain,
and unless they speedily repent, and obtain salvation, they
must perish."—1T 124, 125.

Those Who Indulge and Foster Sin.—Because of
sin, Satan was thrust out of heaven; and no man indulging
and fostering sin can go to heaven, for then Satan would
again have a foothold there.—4T 346.

Heaven Would Be Torture to the Rebellious.—
Could those whose lives have been spent in rebellion against
God be suddenly transported to heaven and witness the
high, the holy state of perfection that ever exists there,—
every soul filled with love, every countenance beaming with
joy, enrapturing music in melodious strains rising in honor
of God and the Lamb, and ceaseless streams of light flowing upon the redeemed from the face of Him who sitteth
upon the throne,—could those whose hearts are filled with
hatred of God, of truth and holiness, mingle with the heavenly throng and join their songs of praise? Could they endure the glory of God and the Lamb? No, no; years of
probation were granted them, that they might form char-

acters for heaven; but they have never trained the mind to love purity; they have never learned the language of heaven, and now it is too late. A life of rebellion against God has unfitted them for heaven. Its purity, holiness, and peace would be torture to them; the glory of God would be a consuming fire. They would long to flee from that holy place. They would welcome destruction, that they might be hidden from the face of Him who died to redeem them. The destiny of the wicked is fixed by their own choice. Their exclusion from heaven is voluntary with themselves, and just and merciful on the part of God.—GC 542, 543.

13

In Heaven One Thousand Years

WICKED REALIZE THEIR LIVES HAVE BEEN A FAILURE.—
When the voice of God turns the captivity of His people,
there is a terrible awakening of those who have lost all in
the great game of life. While probation continued, they
were blinded by Satan's deceptions, and they justified their
course of sin. The rich prided themselves upon their supe-
riority to those who were less favored; but they had ob-
tained their riches by violation of the law of God. They
had neglected to feed the hungry, to clothe the naked, to
deal justly, and to love mercy. They had sought to exalt
themselves, and to obtain the homage of their fellow-
creatures. Now they are stripped of all that made them great,
and are left destitute and defenseless. They look upon the
destruction of the idols which they preferred before their
Maker. They sold their souls for earthly riches and enjoy-
ments, and did not seek to become rich toward God. The

result is, their lives are a failure; their pleasures are now turned to gall, their treasures to corruption. The gain of a lifetime is swept away in a moment.—4SP 470, 471.

WICKED FILLED WITH REGRET.— The wicked are filled with regret, not because of their sinful neglect of God and their fellow men, but because God has conquered. They lament that the result is what it is; but they do not repent of their wickedness. They would leave no means untried to conquer if they could. . . .

No language can express the longing which the disobedient and disloyal feel for that which they have lost forever—eternal life. Men whom the world has worshiped for their talents and eloquence now see these things in their true light. They realize what they have forfeited by transgression, and they fall at the feet of those whose fidelity they have despised and derided, and confess that God has loved them.—GC 654, 655.

WICKED DESTROYED; EARTH DESOLATE.—At the coming of Christ the wicked are blotted from the face of the whole earth—consumed with the spirit of His mouth, and destroyed by the brightness of His glory. Christ takes His people to the city of God, and the earth is emptied of its inhabitants. "Behold, the Lord maketh the earth empty, and maketh it waste, and turneth it upside down, and scattereth abroad the inhabitants thereof." "The land shall be utterly emptied, and utterly spoiled; for the Lord hath spoken this word." "Because they have transgressed the laws, changed the ordinance, broken the everlasting covenant.

Therefore hath the curse devoured the earth, and they that dwell therein are desolate; therefore the inhabitants of the earth are burned." [Isaiah 24:1, 3, 5, 6.]

The whole earth appears like a desolate wilderness. The ruins of cities and villages destroyed by the earthquake, uprooted trees, ragged rocks thrown out by the sea or torn out of the earth itself, are scattered over its surface, while vast caverns mark the spot where the mountains have been rent from their foundations. Here is to be the home of Satan with his evil angels for a thousand years. Here he will be confined, to wander up and down over the broken surface of the earth, and see the effects of his rebellion against the law of God. For a thousand years he can enjoy the fruit of the curse which he has caused. Limited alone to the earth, he will not have the privilege of ranging to other planets, to tempt and annoy those who have not fallen.

During this time, Satan suffers extremely. Since his fall his life of intense activity has banished reflection; but he is now deprived of his power, and left to contemplate the part which he has acted since first he rebelled against the government of Heaven, and to look forward with trembling and terror to the dreadful future, when he must suffer for all the evil that he has done, and be punished for the sins that he has caused to be committed.

Shouts of triumph ascend from the angels and the redeemed saints, that they are to be no more annoyed and tempted by Satan, and that the inhabitants of other worlds are delivered from his presence and temptations.— 4SP 474, 475.

My attention was again directed to the earth. The wicked had been destroyed, and their dead bodies were lying on its surface. The wrath of God in the seven last plagues had been visited upon the inhabitants of the earth, causing them to gnaw their tongues from pain and to curse God. The false shepherds had been the signal objects of Jehovah's wrath. Their eyes had consumed away in their holes, and their tongues in their mouths, while they stood upon their feet. After the saints had been delivered by the voice of God, the wicked multitude turned their rage upon one another. The earth seemed to be deluged with blood, and dead bodies were from one end of it to the other.—SR 415.

JUDGMENT OF WICKED.—During the thousand years between the first and the second resurrection the judgment of the wicked takes place. The apostle Paul points to this judgment as an event that follows the second advent. "Judge nothing before the time, until the Lord come, who both will bring to light the hidden things of darkness, and will make manifest the counsels of the hearts." 1 Corinthians 4:5. Daniel declares that when the Ancient of Days came, "judgment was given to the saints of the Most High." Daniel 7:22. At this time the righteous reign as kings and priests unto God. John in the Revelation says: "I saw thrones, and they sat upon them, and judgment was given unto them." "They shall be priests of God and of Christ, and shall reign with Him a thousand years." Revelation 20:4, 6.

It is at this time that, as foretold by Paul, "the saints shall judge the world." 1 Corinthians 6:2. In union with

Christ they judge the wicked, comparing their acts with the statute book, the Bible, and deciding every case according to the deeds done in the body. Then the portion which the wicked must suffer is meted out, according to their works; and it is recorded against their names in the book of death.

Satan also and evil angels are judged by Christ and His people.—GC 660, 661.

SATAN'S PUNISHMENT COMMENSURATE WITH HIS GUILT.—Satan also and his angels were judged by Jesus and the saints. Satan's punishment was to be far greater than that of those whom he had deceived. His suffering would so far exceed theirs as to bear no comparison with it. After all those whom he had deceived had perished, Satan was still to live and suffer on much longer.—EW 291.

SATAN BANISHED.—Now the event takes place foreshadowed in the last solemn service of the Day of Atonement. When the ministration in the holy of holies had been completed, and the sins of Israel had been removed from the sanctuary by virtue of the blood of the sin offering, then the scapegoat was presented alive before the Lord; and in the presence of the congregation the high priest confessed over him "all the iniquities of the children of Israel, and all their transgressions in all their sins, putting them upon the head of the goat." Leviticus 16:21.

In like manner, when the work of atonement in the heavenly sanctuary has been completed, then in the presence of God and heavenly angels and the hosts of the redeemed the sins of God's people will be placed upon Satan; he will be declared guilty of all the evil which he has caused them to commit. And as the scapegoat was sent away into a land not inhabited, so Satan will be banished to the desolate earth, an uninhabited and dreary wilderness.—GC 658.

14

The End of Evil

JESUS AND THE HOLY CITY DESCEND TO EARTH.—At the end of one thousand years, Jesus, the king of glory, descends from the Holy City, clothed with brightness like the lightning, upon the Mount of Olives—the same mount from whence He ascended after His resurrection. As His feet touch the mountain, it parts asunder, and becomes a very great plain, and is prepared for the reception of the Holy City in which is the paradise of God, the Garden of Eden, which was taken up after man's transgression. Now it descends with the City, more beautiful, and gloriously adorned than when removed from the earth. The City of God comes down and settles upon the mighty plain prepared for it.—3SG 83, 84.

Jesus descended upon a great and mighty mountain, which, as soon as His feet touched it, parted asunder, and became a mighty plain. Then we looked up and saw the great and beautiful City, with twelve foundations, twelve gates, three on each side, and an angel at each gate. We cried out, The City! The great City! It is coming down from God out of heaven! And it came down in all its splendor, and dazzling glory, and settled in the mighty plain which Jesus had prepared for it.—1SG 213.

THE MARKS OF SIN'S CURSE VISIBLE IN THE RESURRECTED WICKED.—Then Jesus in terrible, fearful majesty called forth the wicked dead; and as they came up with the same feeble, sickly bodies that went into the grave, what a spectacle! what a scene! At the first resurrection all came forth in immortal bloom; but at the second, the marks of the curse are visible on all.—1SG 214.

THE FINAL STRUGGLE.—Now Satan prepares for a last mighty struggle for the supremacy. While deprived of his power and cut off from his work of deception, the prince of evil was miserable and dejected; but as the wicked dead are raised and he sees the vast multitudes upon his side, his hopes revive, and he determines not to yield the great controversy. He will marshal all the armies of the lost under his banner and through them endeavor to execute his plans.

The wicked are Satan's captives. In rejecting Christ they have accepted the rule of the rebel leader. They are ready to receive his suggestions and to do his bidding. Yet, true to his early cunning, he does not acknowledge himself to be Satan. He claims to be the prince who is the rightful owner of the world and whose inheritance has been unlawfully wrested from him. He represents himself to his deluded subjects as a redeemer, assuring them that his power has brought them forth from their graves and that he is about to rescue them from the most cruel tyranny.

The presence of Christ having been removed, Satan works wonders to support his claims. He makes the weak strong and inspires all with his own spirit and energy. He proposes to lead them against the camp of the saints and to take possession of the City of God.—GC 663.

SATAN AND HIS FOLLOWERS MARCH AGAINST THE HOLY CITY.—At last the order to advance is given, and the countless host moves on—an army such as was never summoned by earthly conquerors, such as the combined forces of all ages since war began on earth could never equal. Satan, the mightiest of warriors, leads the van, and his angels unite their forces for this final struggle. Kings and warriors are in his train, and the multitudes follow in vast companies, each under its appointed leader. With military precision the serried ranks advance over the earth's broken and uneven surface to the City of God. By command of Jesus, the gates of the New Jerusalem are closed, and the armies of Satan surround the city and make ready for the onset.—GC 664.

THE FINAL CORONATION OF CHRIST TAKES PLACE BE-FORE THE ENTIRE UNIVERSE.—Now Christ again appears to the view of His enemies. Far above the city, upon a foundation of burnished gold, is a throne, high and lifted up. Upon this throne sits the Son of God, and around Him are the subjects of His kingdom. The power and majesty of Christ no language can describe, no pen portray. The glory of the

Eternal Father is enshrouding His Son. The brightness of His presence fills the City of God, and flows out beyond the gates, flooding the whole earth with its radiance.

Nearest the throne are those who were once zealous in the cause of Satan, but who, plucked as brands from the burning, have followed their Saviour with deep, intense devotion. Next are those who perfected Christian characters in the midst of falsehood and infidelity, those who honored the law of God when the Christian world declared it void, and the millions, of all ages, who were martyred for their faith. And beyond is the "great multitude which no man could number, of all nations and kindreds and people and tongues," "before the throne and before the Lamb, clothed with white robes, and palms in their hands." Their warfare is ended, their victory won. They have run the race and reached the prize. The palm branch in their hands is a symbol of their triumph, the white robe an emblem of the spotless righteousness of Christ which now is theirs.

The redeemed raise a song of praise that echoes and re-echoes through the vaults of Heaven, "Salvation to our God which sitteth upon the throne, and unto the Lamb." And angel and seraph unite their voices in adoration. As the redeemed have beheld the power and malignity of Satan, they have seen, as never before, that no power but that of Christ could have made them conquerors. In all that shining throng there are none to ascribe salvation to themselves, as if they had prevailed by their own power and goodness. Nothing is said of what they have done or suffered; but the burden of every song, the keynote of every anthem, is, Salvation to our God and unto the Lamb.

In the presence of the assembled inhabitants of earth and Heaven takes place the final coronation of the Son of God.—4SP 479, 480.

THE WICKED AT GOD'S JUDGMENT BAR.—And now, invested with supreme majesty and power, the King of kings pronounces sentence upon the rebels against His government and executes justice upon those who have transgressed His law and oppressed His people. Says the prophet of God: "I saw a great white throne, and Him that sat on it, from whose face the earth and the heaven fled away; and there was found no place for them. And I saw the dead, small and great, stand before God; and the books were opened: and another book was opened, which is the book of life: and the dead were judged out of those things which were written in the books, according to their works." Revelation 20:11, 12.

As soon as the books of record are opened, and the eye of Jesus looks upon the wicked, they are conscious of every sin which they have ever committed. They see just where their feet diverged from the path of purity and holiness, just how far pride and rebellion have carried them in the violation of the law of God. The seductive temptations which they encouraged by indulgence in sin, the blessings perverted, the messengers of God despised, the warnings rejected, the waves of mercy beaten back by the stubborn, unrepentant heart—all appear as if written in letters of fire. . . .

The whole wicked world stand arraigned at the bar of God on the charge of high treason against the government of heaven. They have none to plead their cause; they are without excuse; and the sentence of eternal death is pronounced against them.

It is now evident to all that the wages of sin is not noble independence and eternal life, but slavery, ruin, and death. The wicked see what they have forfeited by their life of rebellion. The far more exceeding and eternal weight of glory was despised when offered them; but how desirable it now appears. "All this," cries the lost soul, "I might have had; but I chose to put these things far from me. Oh, strange infatuation! I have exchanged peace, happiness, and honor for wretchedness, infamy, and despair." All see that their exclusion from heaven is just. By their lives they have declared: "We will not have this Man [Jesus] to reign over us."—GC 666-668.

SATAN REALIZES HE HAS EXCLUDED HIMSELF FROM HEAVEN.—Satan sees that his voluntary rebellion has unfitted him for heaven. He has trained his powers to war against God; the purity, peace, and harmony of heaven would be to him supreme torture. His accusations against the mercy and justice of God are now silenced. The reproach which he has endeavored to cast upon Jehovah rests wholly upon himself. And now Satan bows down and confesses the justice of his sentence.—GC 670.

THE WICKED ACKNOWLEDGE GOD'S JUSTICE.—As if entranced, the wicked have looked upon the coronation of the Son of God. They see in His hands the tables of the divine law, the statutes which they have despised and transgressed. They witness the outburst of wonder, rapture, and adoration from the saved; and as the wave of melody sweeps over the multitudes without the city, all with one voice exclaim, "Marvelous are thy works, Lord God Almighty; just and true are thy ways, thou King of saints"; and, falling prostrate, they worship the Prince of life.—4SP 484.

GOD IS VINDICATED BEFORE THE UNIVERSE.—Every question of truth and error in the long-standing controversy has now been made plain. The results of rebellion, the fruits of setting aside the divine statutes, have been laid open to the view of all created intelligences. The working out of Satan's rule in contrast with the government of God has been presented to the whole universe. Satan's own works have condemned him. God's wisdom, His justice, and His goodness stand fully vindicated. It is seen that all His dealings in the great controversy have been conducted with respect to the eternal good of His people and the good of all the worlds that He has created. "All Thy works shall praise Thee, O Lord; and Thy saints shall bless Thee." Psalm 145:10.

The history of sin will stand to all eternity as a witness that with the existence of God's law is bound up the happiness of all the beings He has created. With all the facts of the great controversy in view, the whole universe, both loyal and rebellious, with one accord declare: "Just and true are Thy ways, Thou King of saints."—GC 670, 671.

THE WICKED TURN AGAINST SATAN.—Notwithstanding Satan has been constrained to acknowledge God's justice, and to bow to the supremacy of Christ, his character remains unchanged. The spirit of rebellion, like a mighty torrent, again bursts forth. Filled with frenzy, he determines not to yield the great controversy. The time has come for a last desperate struggle against the King of Heaven. He rushes into the midst of his subjects, and endeavors to inspire them with his own fury, and arouse them to instant battle. But of all the countless millions whom he has allured into rebellion, there are none now to acknowledge his supremacy. His power is at an end. The wicked are filled with the same hatred of God that inspires Satan; but they see that their case is hopeless, that they cannot prevail against Jehovah. Their rage is kindled against Satan and those who have been his agents in deception. With the fury of demons they turn upon them, and there follows a scene of universal strife.—4SP 487.

SATAN'S WORK OF RUIN FOREVER ENDED.—The wicked receive their recompense in the earth. Proverbs 11:31. They "shall be stubble: and the day that cometh shall burn them up, saith the Lord of hosts." Malachi 4:1. Some are destroyed as in a moment, while others suffer many days. All are punished "according to their deeds." The sins of the righteous having been transferred to Satan, he is made to suffer not only for his own rebellion, but for all the sins which he has caused God's people to commit. His punishment is to be far greater than that of those whom he has deceived. After all have perished who fell by his deceptions, he is still to live and suffer on. In the cleansing flames the wicked are at last destroyed, root and branch—Satan the root, his followers the branches. The full penalty of the law has been visited;

the demands of justice have been met; and heaven and earth, beholding, declare the righteousness of Jehovah.

Satan's work of ruin is forever ended. For six thousand years he has wrought his will, filling the earth with woe and causing grief throughout the universe. The whole creation has groaned and travailed together in pain. Now God's creatures are forever delivered from his presence and temptations. "The whole earth is at rest, and is quiet: they [the righteous] break forth into singing." Isaiah 14:7. And a shout of praise and triumph ascends from the whole loyal universe. "The voice of a great multitude," "as the voice of many waters, and as the voice of mighty thunderings," is heard, saying: "Alleluia: for the Lord God omnipotent reigneth." Revelation 19:6.—GC 673.

A TERRIBLE MERCY.—It is in mercy to the universe that God will finally destroy the rejecters of His grace.

"The wages of sin is death; but the gift of God is eternal life through Jesus Christ our Lord." Romans 6:23. While life is the inheritance of the righteous, death is the portion of the wicked. Moses declared to Israel: "I have set before thee this day life and good, and death and evil." Deuteronomy 30:15. The death referred to in these scriptures is not that pronounced upon Adam, for all mankind suffer the penalty of his transgression. It is "the second death" that is placed in contrast with everlasting life. . . .

Thus will be made an end of sin, with all the woe and ruin which have resulted from it. Says the psalmist: "Thou hast destroyed the wicked, Thou hast put out their name forever and ever. O thou enemy, destructions are come to a perpetual end." Psalm 9:5, 6. John, in the Revelation, looking forward to the eternal state, hears a universal anthem of praise undisturbed by one note of discord. Every creature in heaven and earth was heard ascribing glory to God. Revelation 5:13. There will then be no lost souls to blaspheme God as they writhe in never-ending torment; no wretched beings in hell will mingle their shrieks with the songs of the saved.—GC 543–545.

THE EARTH PURIFIED BY FIRE.—While the earth was wrapped in the fire of destruction, the righteous abode safely in the Holy City. Upon those that had part in the first resurrection, the second death has no power. While God is to the wicked a consuming fire, He is to His people both a sun and a shield. Revelation 20:6; Psalm 84:11.

"I saw a new heaven and a new earth: for the first heaven and the first earth were passed away." Revelation 21:1. The fire that consumes the wicked purifies the earth. Every trace of the curse is swept away. No eternally burning hell will keep before the ransomed the fearful consequences of sin.—GC 673, 674.

ONLY ONE TRACE OF SIN REMAINS.—One reminder alone remains: Our Redeemer will ever bear the marks of His crucifixion. Upon His wounded head, upon His side, His hands and feet, are the only traces of the cruel work that sin has wrought. Says the prophet, beholding Christ in His glory: "He had bright beams coming out of His side: and there was the hiding of His power." Habakkuk

3:4, margin. That pierced side whence flowed the crimson stream that reconciled man to God—there is the Saviour's glory, there "the hiding of His power." "Mighty to save," through the sacrifice of redemption, He was therefore strong to execute justice upon them that despised God's mercy. And the tokens of His humiliation are His highest honor; through the eternal ages the wounds of Calvary will show forth His praise and declare His power.—GC 674.

CHAPTER

15

The Earth Made New

MORE GLORIOUS THAN WE CAN IMAGINE.—The lion, we should much dread and fear here, will then lie down with the lamb, and everything in the New Earth will be peace and harmony. The trees of the New Earth will be straight and lofty, without deformity.

The saints will have crowns of glory upon their heads, and harps of gold in their hands. They will play upon the golden harp, and sing redeeming love, and make melody unto God. Their former trials and suffering in this world will be forgotten and lost amid the glories of the New Earth.

Let all that is beautiful in our earthly home remind us of the crystal river and green fields, the waving trees and the living fountains, the shining city and the white-robed singers, of our heavenly home—that world of beauty which no artist can picture and no mortal tongue describe. Let your imagination picture the home of the saved, and remember that it will be more glorious than your brightest imagination can portray.

Human language is inadequate to describe the reward of the righteous. It will be known only to those who behold it.—Mar 355.

A fear of making the future inheritance seem too material has led many to spiritualize away the very truths which lead us to look upon it as our home. Christ assured His disciples that He went to prepare mansions for them in the Father's house. Those who accept the teachings of God's Word will not be wholly ignorant concerning the heavenly abode. And yet, "eye hath not seen, nor ear heard, neither have entered into the heart of man, the things which God hath prepared for them that love Him." 1 Corinthians 2:9. Human language is inadequate to describe the reward of the righteous. It will be known only to those who behold it. No finite mind can comprehend the glory of the Paradise of God.—GC 674, 675.

GARDEN OF EDEN RESTORED.—The Garden of Eden remained upon the earth long after man had become an outcast from its pleasant paths. The fallen race were long permitted to gaze upon the home of innocence, their entrance barred only by the watching angels. At the cherubim-guarded gate of Paradise the divine glory was revealed. Hither came Adam and his sons to worship God. Here they renewed their vows of obedience to that law the transgression of which had banished them from Eden. When the tide of iniquity overspread the world, and the wickedness of men determined their destruction by a flood of waters, the hand that had planted Eden withdrew it from the earth. But in the final restitution, when there shall be "a new heaven and a new earth" (Revelation 21:1), it is to be restored more gloriously adorned than at the beginning.

Then they that have kept God's commandments shall breathe in immortal vigor beneath the tree of life; and through unending ages the inhabitants of sinless worlds shall behold, in that garden of delight, a sample of the perfect work of God's creation, untouched by the curse of sin—a sample of what the whole earth would have become had man but fulfilled the Creator's glorious plan.—PP 62.

THE REDEEMED WILL GROW PHYSICALLY TO THEIR "FULL STATURE."—All blemishes and deformities are left in the grave. Restored to the tree of life in the long-lost Eden, the redeemed will "grow up" (Malachi 4:2) to the full stature of the race in its primeval glory. The last lingering traces of the curse of sin will be removed, and Christ's faithful ones will appear in "the beauty of the Lord our God," in mind and soul and body reflecting the perfect image of their Lord. Oh, wonderful redemption! long talked of, long hoped for, contemplated with eager anticipation, but never fully understood.—GC 645.

MRS. WHITE'S VISION OF THE NEW EARTH.—With Jesus at our head we all descended from the City down to this earth, on a great and mighty mountain, which could not bear Jesus up, and it parted asunder, and there was a mighty plain. Then we looked up and saw the great City, with twelve foundations, twelve gates, three on each side, and an angel at each gate. We all cried out, "The City, the great City, it's coming! It's coming down from God out of heaven!" And it came and settled on the place where we stood.

Then we began to look at the glorious things outside of the City. There I saw most beautiful houses, that had the appearance of silver, supported by four pillars set with pearls, most glorious to behold, which were to be inhabited by the saints, and in them was a golden shelf. I saw many of the saints go into the houses, take off their glittering crowns and lay them on the shelf, then go out into the field by the houses to do something with the earth; not as we have to do with the earth here. A glorious light shone all about their heads, and they were continually offering praises to God.

And I saw another field full of all kinds of flowers, and as I plucked them I cried out, They will never fade. Next I saw a field of tall grass most glorious to behold; it was living green, and had a reflection of silver and gold, as it waved to the glory of King Jesus. Then we entered a field full of all kinds of beasts—the lion, the lamb, the leopard and the wolf, all together in perfect union. We passed through the midst of them, and they followed on peaceably after. Then we entered a wood, not like the dark woods we have here; but light and beautiful. The branches of the trees waved to and fro, and we all cried out, "We will dwell safely in the wilderness and sleep in the woods."

We passed through the woods, for we were on our way to Mount Zion. As we were traveling along, we met a company who were also gazing at the glories of the place. I noticed red as a border on their garments; their crowns were brilliant; their robes were pure white. As we greeted them I asked Jesus who they were. He said they were martyrs that had been slain for Him. With them was an innumerable company of little ones; they had a hem of red on their garments also.

Mount Zion was just before us, and on the mount was a building which looked to me like a temple, and about it were seven other mountains, on which grew roses and lilies. And I saw the little ones climb, or if they chose, use their little wings and fly to the top of the mountains, and pluck the never-fading flowers. There were all kinds of trees to beautify the place; the box, the pine, the fir, the oil, the myrtle, the pomegranate, and the fig-tree, bowed down with the weight of its timely figs, that made the place all over glorious. And as we were about to enter the temple, Jesus raised His lovely voice and said, Only the 144,000 enter this place, and we shouted Alleluia.

The temple was supported by seven pillars, all of transparent gold, set with pearls most glorious. The things I saw there I cannot describe. Oh that I could talk in the language of Canaan, then could I tell a little of the glory of the better world. I saw there tables of stone in which the names of 144,000 were engraved in letters of gold. After we beheld the glory of the temple, we went out, and Jesus left us, and went to the City. Soon we heard His lovely voice again, saying, "Come, My people, you have come out of great tribulation, and done My will; suffered for Me; come in to supper; for I will gird Myself and serve you." We shouted Alleluia, glory, and entered into the City.

And I saw a table of pure silver, it was many miles in

length, yet our eyes could extend over it. I saw the fruit of the tree of life, the manna, almonds, figs, pomegranates, grapes, and many other kinds of fruit. I asked Jesus to let me eat of the fruit. He said, Not now. Those who eat of the fruit of this land, go back to earth no more. But in a little while, if faithful, you shall both eat of the fruit of the tree of life, and drink of the water of the fountain. And He said, You must go back to earth again, and relate to others what I have revealed to you. Then an angel bore me gently down to this dark world.—2SG 52-55.

IN HEAVEN, ALL IS PURITY AND PEACE.—Through Christ alone can you make sure of heaven, where all is purity, holiness, peace, and blessedness, where there are glories that mortal lips cannot describe. The nearest we can come to a description of the reward that awaits the overcomer is to say that it is a far more exceeding and eternal weight of glory. It will be an eternity of bliss, a blessed eternity, unfolding new glories throughout the ceaseless ages.—8T 131.

NO TREE OF KNOWLEDGE IN THE NEW EARTH.—Not all the conditions of that first school of Eden will be found in the school of the future life. No tree of knowledge of good and evil will afford opportunity for temptation. No tempter is there, no possibility of wrong. Every character has withstood the testing of evil, and none are longer susceptible to its power.—Ed 302.

NO SEA.—The sea divides friends. It is a barrier between us and those whom we love. Our associations are broken up by the broad, fathomless ocean. In the New Earth there will be no more sea, and there shall pass there "no galley with oars." In the past many who have loved and served God have been bound by chains to their seats in galleys, compelled to serve the purpose of cruel, hardhearted men. The Lord has looked upon their suffering in sympathy and compassion. Thank God, in the earth made new there will be no fierce torrents, no engulfing ocean, no restless, murmuring waves.—Ms 33, 1911 quoted in Mar 351.

NO TEARS OR FUNERALS.—In the home of the redeemed there will be no tears, no funeral trains, no badges of mourning. "The inhabitant shall not say, I am sick: the people that dwell therein shall be forgiven their iniquity." Isaiah 33:24. One rich tide of happiness will flow and deepen as eternity rolls on. . . .

Let us consider most earnestly the blessed hereafter. Let our faith pierce through every cloud of darkness and behold Him who died for the sins of the world. He has opened the gates of paradise to all who receive and believe on Him. To them He gives power to become the sons and daughters of God. Let the afflictions which pain us so grievously become instructive lessons, teaching us to press forward toward the mark of the prize of our high calling in Christ. Let us be encouraged by the thought that the Lord is soon to come. Let this hope gladden our hearts. . . .

We are homeward bound. He who loved us so much as to die for us hath builded for us a city. The New Jerusalem is our place of rest. There will be no sadness in the city of God. No wail of sorrow, no dirge of crushed hopes and buried affections, will evermore be heard. Soon the garments of heaviness will be changed for the wedding garment. Soon we shall witness the coronation of our King. Those whose lives have been hidden with Christ, those who on this earth have fought the good fight of faith, will shine forth with the Redeemer's glory in the kingdom of God. —9T 286, 287 quoted in Mar 352.

No Marriages or Births.—There are men today who express their belief that there will be marriages and births in the New Earth, but those who believe the Scriptures cannot accept such doctrines. The doctrine that children will be born in the New Earth is not a part of the "sure word of prophecy." The words of Christ are too plain to be misunderstood. They should forever settle the question of marriages and births in the New Earth. Neither those who shall be raised from the dead, nor those who shall be translated without seeing death, will marry or be given in marriage. They will be as the angels of God, members of the royal family.—Ms 28, 1904 quoted in Mar 369.

No Night or Need of Rest.—In the City of God "there shall be no night." None will need or desire repose. There will be no weariness in doing the will of God and offering praise to His name. We shall ever feel the freshness of the morning and shall ever be far from its close. "And they need no candle, neither light of the sun; for the Lord God giveth them light." Revelation 22:5. The light of the sun will be superseded by a radiance which is not painfully dazzling, yet which immeasurably surpasses the brightness of our noontide. The glory of God and the Lamb floods the Holy City with unfading light. The redeemed walk in the sunless glory of perpetual day.—GC 676.

No Temple, But Face-to-Face Communion.—"I saw no temple therein: for the Lord God Almighty and the Lamb are the temple of it." Revelation 21:22. The people of God are privileged to hold open communion with the Father and the Son. "Now we see through a glass, darkly." 1 Corinthians 13:12. We behold the image of God reflected, as in a mirror, in the works of nature and in His dealings with men; but then we shall see Him face to face, without a dimming veil between. We shall stand in His presence and behold the glory of His countenance.—GC 676, 677.

No Pain, Sickness, or Death.—Oh, I long for Jesus to come. I long for that home in the kingdom of glory where there will be no sickness, no sorrow, no pain, no death.—Letter 64a, 1889 quoted in 10MR 383.

No Contention or Discord.—No voices of contention mar the sweet and perfect peace of heaven. Its inhabitants know no sorrow, no grief, no tears. All is in perfect harmony, in perfect order and perfect bliss. . . .

Heaven is a home where sympathy is alive in every heart, expressed in every look. Love reigns there. There are no jarring elements, no discord or contentions or war of words.—Letter 30, 1882 quoted in LDE 296.

THE SABBATH WILL CONTINUE TO BE OBSERVED IN THE NEW EARTH.—I was shown that the law of God would stand fast forever, and exist in the new earth to all eternity. At the creation, when the foundations of the earth were laid, the sons of God looked with admiration upon the work of the Creator, and all the heavenly host shouted for joy. It was then that the foundation of the Sabbath was laid. At the close of the six days of creation, God rested on the seventh day from all His work which He had made; and He blessed the seventh day and sanctified it, because that in it He had rested from all His work.

The Sabbath was instituted in Eden before the fall, and was observed by Adam and Eve, and all the heavenly host. God rested on the seventh day, and blessed and hallowed it. I saw that the Sabbath never will be done away; but that the redeemed saints, and all the angelic host, will observe it in honor of the great Creator to all eternity.—EW 217.

The Sabbath was not for Israel merely, but for the world. It had been made known to man in Eden, and, like the other precepts of the Decalogue, it is of imperishable obligation. Of that law of which the fourth commandment forms a part, Christ declares, "Till heaven and earth pass, one jot or one tittle shall in no wise pass from the law." Matthew 5:18. So long as the heavens and the earth endure, the Sabbath will continue as a sign of the Creator's power. And when Eden shall bloom on earth again, God's holy rest day will be honored by all beneath the sun. "From one sabbath to another" the inhabitants of the glorified new earth shall . . . "worship before me, saith the Lord."—DA 283 quoted in FLB 37.

COMMUNION WITH THE FAITHFUL OF ALL AGES.—There the redeemed shall know, even as also they are known. The loves and sympathies which God Himself has planted in the soul shall there find truest and sweetest exercise. The pure communion with holy beings, the harmonious social life with the blessed angels and with the faithful ones of all ages who have washed their robes and made them white in the blood of the Lamb, the sacred ties that bind together "the whole family in heaven and earth" (Ephesians 3:15)—these help to constitute the happiness of the redeemed.—GC 677.

THE HAPPINESS OF OTHERS IS THE JOY OF THE REDEEMED.—Everything in heaven is noble and elevated. All seek the interest and happiness of others. No one devotes himself to looking out and caring for self. It is the chief joy of all holy beings to witness the joy and happiness of those around them.—2T 239.

GOD'S PEOPLE ARE AT HOME IN THE NEW EARTH.—In the Bible the inheritance of the saved is called "a country." Hebrews 11:14-16. There the heavenly Shepherd leads His flock to fountains of living waters. The tree of life yields its fruit every month, and the leaves of the tree are for the service of the nations. There are ever-flowing streams, clear as crystal, and beside them waving trees cast their shadows upon the paths prepared for the ransomed of the Lord. There the wide-spreading plains swell into hills of beauty, and the mountains of God rear their lofty summits. On those peaceful plains, beside those living streams, God's people, so long pilgrims and wanderers, shall find a home.

"My people shall dwell in a peaceable habitation, and in sure dwellings, and in quiet resting places." "Violence shall no more be heard in thy land, wasting nor destruction within thy borders; but thou shalt call thy walls Salvation, and thy gates Praise." "They shall build houses, and inhabit them; and they shall plant vineyards, and eat the fruit of them. They shall not build, and another inhabit; they shall not plant, and another eat: . . . Mine elect shall long enjoy the work of their hands." Isaiah 32:18; 60:18; 65:21, 22.

There, "the wilderness and the solitary place shall be glad for them; and the desert shall rejoice, and blossom as the rose." "Instead of the thorn shall come up the fir tree, and instead of the brier shall come up the myrtle tree." "The wolf also shall dwell with the lamb, and the leopard shall lie down with the kid; . . . and a little child shall lead them." "They shall not hurt nor destroy in all My holy mountain," saith the Lord. Isaiah 35:1; 55:13; 11:6, 9. —GC 675, 676.

THE REDEEMED WILL LIVE ACTIVE, PURPOSEFUL LIVES.— In the earth made new the redeemed will engage in the occupations and pleasures that brought happiness to Adam and Eve in the beginning. The Eden life will be lived, the life in garden and field. "They shall build houses, and inhabit them; and they shall plant vineyards, and eat the fruit of them. They shall not build, and another inhabit; they shall not plant, and another eat: for as the days of a tree are the days of My people, and Mine elect shall long enjoy the work of their hands."—PK 730, 731 quoted in AH 549.

There every power will be developed, every capability increased. The grandest enterprises will be carried forward, the loftiest aspirations will be reached, the highest ambitions realized. And still there will arise new heights to surmount, new wonders to admire, new truths to comprehend, fresh objects to call forth the powers of body and mind and soul.—Ed 306 quoted in AH 549.

CHAPTER

16

Heaven Is a School

ETERNITY WILL PROVIDE ENDLESS OPPORTUNITY FOR LEARNING AND GROWTH.—Heaven is a school; its field of study, the universe; its teacher, the Infinite One. A branch of this school was established in Eden; and, the plan of redemption accomplished, education will again be taken up in the Eden school.

"Eye hath not seen, nor ear heard, neither have entered into the heart of man, the things which God hath prepared for them that love Him." 1 Corinthians 2:9. Only through His Word can a knowledge of these things be gained; and even this affords but a partial revelation.

The prophet of Patmos thus describes the location of the school of the hereafter:

"I saw a new heaven and a new earth: for the first heaven and the first earth were passed away. . . . And I John saw the Holy City, New Jerusalem, coming down from God out of heaven, prepared as a bride adorned for her husband." Revelation 21:1, 2.

"The city had no need of the sun, neither of the moon, to shine in it: for the glory of God did lighten it, and the Lamb is the light thereof." Revelation 21:23.

Between the school established in Eden at the beginning and the school of the hereafter there lies the whole compass of this world's history—the history of human transgression and suffering, of divine sacrifice, and of victory over death and sin. Not all the conditions of that first school of Eden will be found in the school of the future life. No tree of knowledge of good and evil will afford opportunity for temptation. No tempter is there, no possibility of wrong. Every character has withstood the testing of evil, and none are longer susceptible to its power.

"To him that overcometh," Christ says, "will I give to eat of the tree of life, which is in the midst of the Paradise of God." Revelation 2:7. The giving of the tree of life in Eden was conditional, and it was finally withdrawn. But the gifts of the future life are absolute and eternal.

The prophet beholds the "river of water of life, clear as crystal, proceeding out of the throne of God and of the Lamb." "And on this side of the river and on that was the tree of life." "And there shall be no more death, neither sorrow, nor crying, neither shall there be any more pain: for the former things are passed away." Revelation 22:1; 22:2, R.V.; 21:4.

"Thy people also shall be all righteous:
They shall inherit the land forever,
The branch of My planting,
The work of My hands,

That I may be glorified." Isaiah 60:21.

Restored to His presence, man will again, as at the beginning, be taught of God: "My people shall know My name: . . . they shall know in that day that I am He that doth speak: behold, it is I." Isaiah 52:6.

"The tabernacle of God is with men, and He will dwell with them, and they shall be His people, and God Himself shall be with them, and be their God." Revelation 21:3.

"These are they which came out of great tribulation, and have washed their robes, and made them white in the blood of the Lamb. Therefore are they before the throne of God, and serve Him day and night in His temple. . . . They shall hunger no more, neither thirst any more; neither shall the sun light on them, nor any heat. For the Lamb which is in the midst of the throne shall feed them, and shall lead them unto living fountains of waters." Revelation 7:14-17.

"Now we see through a glass, darkly; but then face to face:" now we know in part; but then shall we know even as also we are known. 1 Corinthians 13:12.

"They shall see His face; and His name shall be in their foreheads." Revelation 22:4.

There, when the veil that darkens our vision shall be removed, and our eyes shall behold that world of beauty of which we now catch glimpses through the microscope; when we look on the glories of the heavens, now scanned afar through the telescope; when, the blight of sin removed, the whole earth shall appear in "the beauty of the Lord our God," what a field will be open to our study! There the student of science may read the records of creation and discern no reminders of the law of evil. He may listen to the music of nature's voices and detect no note of wailing or undertone of sorrow. In all created things he may trace one handwriting— in the vast universe behold "God's name writ large," and not in earth or sea or sky one sign of ill remaining.

There the Eden life will be lived, the life in garden and field. "They shall build houses, and inhabit them; and they shall plant vineyards, and eat the fruit of them. They shall not build, and another inhabit; they shall not plant, and another eat: for as the days of a tree are the days of My people, and Mine elect shall long enjoy the work of their hands." Isaiah 65:21, 22.

There shall be nothing to "hurt nor destroy in all My holy mountain, saith the Lord." Isaiah 65:25. There man will be restored to his lost kingship, and the lower order of beings will again recognize his sway; the fierce will become gentle, and the timid trustful.

There will be open to the student, history of infinite scope and of wealth inexpressible. Here, from the vantage ground of God's Word, the student is afforded a view of the vast field of history and may gain some knowledge of the principles that govern the course of human events. But his vision is still clouded, and his knowledge incomplete. Not until he stands in the light of eternity will he see all things clearly.

Then will be opened before him the course of the great conflict that had its birth before time began, and that ends only when time shall cease. The history of the inception of sin; of fatal falsehood in its crooked working; of truth that, swerving not from its own straight lines, has met and conquered error—all will be made manifest. The veil that interposes between the visible and the invisible world will be drawn aside, and wonderful things will be revealed.

Not until the providences of God are seen in the light of eternity shall we understand what we owe to the care and interposition of His angels. Celestial beings have taken an active part in the affairs of men. They have appeared in garments that shone as the lightning; they have come as men, in the garb of wayfarers. They have accepted the hospitalities of human homes; they have acted as guides to benighted travelers. They have thwarted the spoiler's purpose and turned aside the stroke of the destroyer.

Though the rulers of this world know it not, yet often in their councils angels have been spokesmen. Human eyes have looked upon them. Human ears have listened to their appeals. In the council hall and the court of justice, heavenly messengers have pleaded the cause of the persecuted and oppressed. They have defeated purposes and arrested evils that would have brought wrong and suffering to God's children. To the students in the heavenly school, all this will be unfolded.

Every redeemed one will understand the ministry of angels in his own life. The angel who was his guardian from his earliest moment; the angel who watched his steps, and covered his head in the day of peril; the angel who was with him in the valley of the shadow of death, who marked his resting place, who was the first to greet him in the resurrection morning—what will it be to hold converse with him, and to learn the history of divine interposition in the individual life, of heavenly cooperation in every work for humanity!

All the perplexities of life's experience will then be made

plain. Where to us have appeared only confusion and disappointment, broken purposes and thwarted plans, will be seen a grand, overruling, victorious purpose, a divine harmony.

There all who have wrought with unselfish spirit will behold the fruit of their labors. The outworking of every right principle and noble deed will be seen. Something of this we see here. But how little of the result of the world's noblest work is in this life manifest to the doer!

How many toil unselfishly and unweariedly for those who pass beyond their reach and knowledge! Parents and teachers lie down in their last sleep, their lifework seeming to have been wrought in vain; they know not that their faithfulness has unsealed springs of blessing that can never cease to flow; only by faith they see the children they have trained become a benediction and an inspiration to their fellow men, and the influence repeat itself a thousandfold. Many a worker sends out into the world messages of strength and hope and courage, words that carry blessing to hearts in every land; but of the results he, toiling in loneliness and obscurity, knows little. So gifts are bestowed, burdens are borne, labor is done. Men sow the seed from which, above their graves, others reap blessed harvests. They plant trees, that others may eat the fruit. They are content here to know that they have set in motion agencies for good. In the hereafter the action and reaction of all these will be seen.

Of every gift that God has bestowed, leading men to unselfish effort, a record is kept in heaven. To trace this in its wide-spreading lines, to look upon those who by our efforts have been uplifted and ennobled, to behold in their history the outworking of true principles—this will be one of the studies and rewards of the heavenly school.

There we shall know even as also we are known. There the loves and sympathies that God has planted in the soul will find truest and sweetest exercise. The pure communion with holy beings, the harmonious social life with the blessed angels and with the faithful ones of all ages, the sacred fellowship that binds together "the whole family in heaven and earth"—all are among the experiences of the hereafter.

There will be music there, and song, such music and song as, save in the visions of God, no mortal ear has heard or mind conceived.

"As well the singers as the players on instruments shall be there." Psalm 87:7. "They shall lift up their voice, they shall sing for the majesty of the Lord." Isaiah 24:14.

"For the Lord shall comfort Zion: He will comfort all her waste places; and He will make her wilderness like Eden, and her desert like the garden of the Lord; joy and gladness shall be found therein, thanksgiving, and the voice of melody." Isaiah 51:3.

There every power will be developed, every capability increased. The grandest enterprises will be carried forward, the loftiest aspirations will be reached, the highest ambitions realized. And still there will arise new heights to surmount, new wonders to admire, new truths to comprehend, fresh objects to call forth the powers of body and mind and soul.

All the treasures of the universe will be open to the study of God's children. With unutterable delight we shall enter into the joy and the wisdom of unfallen beings. We shall share the treasures gained through ages upon ages spent in contemplation of God's handiwork. And the years of eternity, as they roll, will continue to bring more glorious revelations. "Exceeding abundantly above all that we ask or think" (Ephesians 3:20) will be, forever and forever, the impartation of the gifts of God.

"His servants shall serve Him." Revelation 22:3. The life on earth is the beginning of the life in heaven; education on earth is an initiation into the principles of heaven; the lifework here is a training for the lifework there. What we now are, in character and holy service, is the sure foreshadowing of what we shall be.

"The Son of man came not to be ministered unto, but to minister." Matthew 20:28. Christ's work below is His work above, and our reward for working with Him in this world will be the greater power and wider privilege of working with Him in the world to come.

"Ye are My witnesses, saith the Lord, that I am God." Isaiah 43:12. This also we shall be in eternity.

For what was the great controversy permitted to continue throughout the ages? Why was it that Satan's existence was not cut short at the outset of his rebellion? It was that the universe might be convinced of God's justice in His dealing with evil; that sin might receive eternal condemnation. In the plan of redemption there are heights and depths that eternity itself can never exhaust, marvels into which the angels desire to look. The redeemed only, of all created beings, have in their own experience known the actual conflict with sin; they have wrought with Christ, and, as even the angels could not do, have entered into the fellowship of His sufferings; will they have no testimony as to the science of redemption—nothing that will be of worth to unfallen beings?

Even now, "unto the principalities and the powers in the heavenly places" is "made known through the church the manifold wisdom of God." And He "hath raised us up together, and made us sit together in heavenly places: . . . that in the ages to come He might show the exceeding riches of His grace in His kindness toward us through Christ Jesus." Ephesians 3:10, R.V.; 2:6, 7.

"In His temple doth everyone speak of His glory" (Psalm 29:9), and the song which the ransomed ones will sing—the song of their experience—will declare the glory of God: "Great and marvelous are Thy works, O Lord God, the Almighty; righteous and true are Thy ways, Thou King of the ages. Who shall not fear, O Lord, and glorify Thy name? for Thou only art holy." Revelation 15:3, 4, R.V.

In our life here, earthly, sin-restricted though it is, the greatest joy and the highest education are in service. And in the future state, untrammeled by the limitations of sinful humanity, it is in service that our greatest joy and our highest education will be found—witnessing, and ever as we witness learning anew "the riches of the glory of this mystery;" "which is Christ in you, the hope of glory." Colossians 1:27.

"It doth not yet appear what we shall be: but we know that, when He shall appear, we shall be like Him; for we shall see Him as He is." 1 John 3:2.

Then, in the results of His work, Christ will behold its recompense. In that great multitude which no man could number, presented "faultless before the presence of His glory with exceeding joy" (Jude 24), He whose blood has redeemed and whose life has taught us, "shall see of the travail of His soul, and shall be satisfied." Isaiah 53:11.—Ed 301-309.

CHRIST WILL BE OUR TEACHER.—Do you think we shall not learn anything there? We have not the slightest idea of what will then be opened before us. With Christ we shall walk beside the living waters. He will unfold to us the beauty and glory of nature. He will reveal what He is to us and what we are to Him. Truth we cannot know now because of finite limitations, we shall know hereafter.—CT 162 quoted in AH 547.

HEAVENLY KNOWLEDGE WILL BE PROGRESSIVE.—All the treasures of the universe will be open to the study of God's redeemed. Unfettered by mortality, they wing their tireless flight to worlds afar—worlds that thrilled with sorrow at the spectacle of human woe and rang with songs of gladness at the tidings of a ransomed soul. With unutterable delight the children of earth enter into the joy and the wisdom of unfallen beings. They share the treasures of knowledge and understanding gained through the ages upon ages in contemplation of God's handiwork. With undimmed vision they gaze upon the glory of creation—suns and stars and systems, all in their appointed order circling the throne of Deity. Upon all things, from the least to the greatest, the Creator's name is written, and in all are the riches of His power displayed.—GC 677, 678.

And the years of eternity, as they roll, will bring richer and still more glorious revelations of God and of Christ. As knowledge is progressive, so will love, reverence, and happiness increase. The more men learn of God, the greater will be their admiration of His character.—GC 678.

HIGHER EDUCATION IN THE FUTURE LIFE.—Christ, the heavenly Teacher, will lead His people to the tree of life that grows on either side of the river of life, and He will explain to them the truths they could not in this life understand. In that future life His people will gain the higher education in its completeness. Those who enter the city of God will have the golden crowns placed upon their heads. That will be a joyful scene that none of us can afford to miss. We shall cast our crowns at the feet of Jesus, and again and again we will give Him the glory and praise His holy name. Angels will unite in the songs of triumph. Touching their golden harps, they will fill all heaven with rich music and songs to the Lamb.—Ms 31, 1909 quoted in 7BC 988.

PLAN OF REDEMPTION WILL CONTINUALLY UNFOLD.— In this life we can only begin to understand the wonderful theme of redemption. With our finite comprehension we may consider most earnestly the shame and the glory, the life and the death, the justice and the mercy, that meet in the cross; yet with the utmost stretch of our mental powers we fail to grasp its full significance. The length and the breadth, the depth and the height, of redeeming love are but dimly comprehended. The plan of redemption will not be fully understood, even when the ransomed see as they are seen and know as they are known; but through the eternal ages new truth will continually unfold to the wondering and delighted mind. Though the griefs and pains and temptations of earth are ended and the cause removed, the people of God will ever have a distinct, intelligent knowledge of what their salvation has cost.

The cross of Christ will be the science and the song of the redeemed through all eternity. In Christ glorified they will behold Christ crucified. Never will it be forgotten that He whose power created and upheld the unnumbered worlds through the vast realms of space, the Beloved of God, the Majesty of heaven, He whom cherub and shining seraph delighted to adore—humbled Himself to uplift fallen man; that He bore the guilt and shame of sin, and the hiding of His Father's face, till the woes of a lost world broke His heart and crushed out His life on Calvary's cross.

That the Maker of all worlds, the Arbiter of all destinies, should lay aside His glory and humiliate Himself from love to man will ever excite the wonder and adoration of the universe. As the nations of the saved look upon their Redeemer and behold the eternal glory of the Father shining in His countenance; as they behold His throne, which is from everlasting to everlasting, and know that His kingdom is to have no end, they break forth in rapturous song: "Worthy, worthy is the Lamb that was slain, and hath redeemed us to God by His own most precious blood!"—GC 651, 652.

ETERNITY CANNOT FULLY REVEAL GOD'S LOVE.—All the paternal love which has come down from generation to generation through the channel of human hearts, all the springs of tenderness which have opened in the souls of men, are but as a tiny rill to the boundless ocean when compared with the infinite, exhaustless love of God. Tongue cannot utter it; pen cannot portray it. You may meditate upon it every day of your life; you may search the Scriptures diligently in order to understand it; you may summon every power and capability that God has given you, in the endeavor to comprehend the love and compassion of the heavenly Father; and yet there is an infinity beyond.

You may study that love for ages; yet you can never fully comprehend the length and the breadth, the depth and the height, of the love of God in giving His Son to die for the world. Eternity itself can never fully reveal it. Yet as we study the Bible and meditate upon the life of Christ and the plan of redemption, these great themes will open to our understanding more and more. And it will be ours to realize the blessing which Paul desired for the Ephesian church when he prayed "that the God of our Lord Jesus Christ, the Father of glory, may give unto you the Spirit of wisdom and revelation in the knowledge of Him; the eyes of your understanding being enlightened, that ye may know what is the hope of His calling, and what the riches of the glory of His inheritance in the saints, and what is the exceeding greatness of His power to usward who believe."—5T 740.

17

It Will Not Be Long

WE ARE HOMEWARD BOUND.—The resurrection and ascension of our Lord is a sure evidence of the triumph of the saints of God over death and the grave, and a pledge that heaven is open to those who wash their robes of character and make them white in the blood of the Lamb. Jesus ascended to the Father as a representative of the human race, and God will bring those who reflect His image to behold and share with Him His glory.

There are homes for the pilgrims of earth. There are robes for the righteous, with crowns of glory and palms of victory. All that has perplexed us in the providences of God will in the world to come be made plain. The things hard to be understood will then find explanation. The mysteries of grace will unfold before us. Where our finite minds discovered only confusion and broken promises, we shall see the most perfect and beautiful harmony. We shall know that infinite love ordered the experiences that seemed most trying. As we realize the tender care of Him who makes all things work together for our good, we shall rejoice with joy unspeakable and full of glory.

Pain cannot exist in the atmosphere of heaven. In the home of the redeemed there will be no tears, no funeral trains, no badges of mourning. "The inhabitant shall not say, I am sick: the people that dwell therein shall be forgiven their iniquity." Isaiah 33:24. One rich tide of happiness will flow and deepen as eternity rolls on.

We are still amidst the shadows and turmoil of earthly activities. Let us consider most earnestly the blessed hereafter. Let our faith pierce through every cloud of darkness and behold Him who died for the sins of the world. He has opened the gates of paradise to all who receive and believe on Him. To them He gives power to become the sons and daughters of God. Let the afflictions which pain us so grievously become instructive lessons, teaching us to press forward toward the mark of the prize of our high calling in Christ. Let us be encouraged by the thought that the Lord is soon to come. Let this hope gladden our hearts. "Yet a little while, and He that shall come will come, and will not tarry." Hebrews 10:37. Blessed are those servants who, when their Lord comes, shall be found watching.

We are homeward bound. He who loved us so much as to die for us hath builded for us a city. The New Jerusalem is our place of rest. There will be no sadness in the city of God. No wail of sorrow, no dirge of crushed hopes and buried affections, will evermore be heard. Soon the garments of heaviness will be changed for the wedding garment. Soon we shall witness the coronation of our King. Those whose lives have been hidden with Christ, those who on this earth have fought the good fight of faith, will shine forth with the Redeemer's glory in the kingdom of God.

It will not be long till we shall see Him in whom our hopes of eternal life are centered. And in His presence, all the trials and sufferings of this life will be as nothingness. "Cast not away therefore your confidence, which hath great recompense of reward. For ye have need of patience, that, after ye have done the will of God, ye might receive the promise. For yet a little while, and He that shall come will come, and will not tarry." Verses 35-37.

Look up, look up, and let your faith continually increase. Let this faith guide you along the narrow path that leads through the gates of the city of God into the great beyond, the wide, unbounded future of glory that is for the redeemed. "Be patient therefore, brethren, unto the coming of the Lord. Behold, the husbandman waiteth for the precious fruit of the earth, and hath long patience for it, until he receive the early and latter rain. Be ye also patient; stablish your hearts: for the coming of the Lord draweth nigh." James 5:7, 8.—9T 286-288.

WE CAN HASTEN HIS COMING.—Christ tells us when the day of His kingdom shall be ushered in. He does not say that all the world will be converted, but that "this gospel of the kingdom shall be preached in all the world for a witness unto all nations; and then shall the end come" (Matthew 24:14). By giving the gospel to the world, it is in our power to hasten the coming of the day of God. Had the church of

Christ done her appointed work as the Lord ordained, the whole world would before this have been warned, and the Lord Jesus would have come to the earth in power and great glory.—RH November 13, 1913 quoted in AG 353.

A LITTLE LONGER.—Christ is coming with clouds and with great glory. A multitude of shining angels will attend Him. He will come to raise the dead, and to change the living saints from glory to glory. He will come to honor those who have loved Him, and kept His commandments, and to take them to Himself. He has not forgotten them nor His promise. There will be a relinking of the family chain. When we look upon our dead, we may think of the morning when the trump of God shall sound, when "the dead shall be raised incorruptible, and we shall be changed." 1 Corinthians 15:52.

A little longer, and we shall see the King in His beauty. A little longer, and He will wipe all tears from our eyes. A little longer, and He will present us "faultless before the presence of His glory with exceeding joy." Jude 24. Wherefore, when He gave the signs of His coming He said, "When these things begin to come to pass, then look up, and lift up your heads; for your redemption draweth nigh."—DA 632.

ONLY A LITTLE WHILE.—It will only be a little while before Jesus will come to save His children and to give them the finishing touch of immortality. "This corruptible shall have put on incorruption, and this mortal shall have put on immortality." The graves will be opened, and the dead will come forth victorious, crying, "O death, where is thy sting? O grave, where is thy victory?" Our loved ones who sleep in Jesus will come forth clothed with immortality.

And as the redeemed shall ascend to heaven, the gates of the city of God will swing back, and those who have kept the truth will enter in. A voice, richer than any music that ever fell on mortal ear, will be heard saying, "Come, ye blessed of My Father, inherit the kingdom prepared for you from the foundation of the world." Then the righteous will receive their reward. Their lives will run parallel with the life of Jehovah. They will cast their crowns at the Redeemer's feet, touch the golden harps, and fill all heaven with rich music.—ST April 15, 1889 quoted in CS 350.

THE END IS AT HAND.—The coming of the Lord is nearer than when we first believed. The great controversy is nearing its end. Every report of calamity by sea or land is a testimony to the fact that the end of all things is at hand. Wars and rumors of wars declare it. Is there a Christian whose pulse does not beat with quickened action as he anticipates the great events opening before us?—RH November 12, 1914 quoted in Ev 219.

SURE IS THE PROMISE.—"Let not your heart be troubled: ye believe in God, believe also in Me. In My Father's house are many mansions: if it were not so, I would have told you. I go to prepare a place for you. And if I go and prepare a place for you, I will come again, and receive you unto Myself; that where I am, there ye may be also." John 14:1-3.

Long have we waited for our Saviour's return. But nonetheless sure is the promise. Soon we shall be in our promised home.

There Jesus will lead us beside the living stream flowing from the throne of God and will explain to us the dark providences through which on this earth He brought us in order to perfect our characters. There we shall behold with undimmed vision the beauties of Eden restored. Casting at the feet of the Redeemer the crowns that He has placed on our heads, and touching our golden harps, we shall fill all heaven with praise to Him that sitteth on the throne.—8T 254.

DWELL ON HIS COMING.—Dwell on present truth, on Christ's second coming. The Lord is coming very soon. We have only a little while in which to present the truth for this time—the truth that is to convert souls. This truth is to be presented in the utmost simplicity, even as Christ presented it, so that the people can understand what is truth. Truth will dispel the clouds of error.—Letter 175, 1904 quoted in Ev 624.

ESSENTIAL PART OF GOSPEL.—The preaching of Christ's second coming, the announcement of its nearness, is shown to be an essential part of the gospel message.—COL 227, 228.

THE LAST CALL.—God has called this people to give to the world the message of Christ's soon coming. We are to give to men the last call to the gospel feast, the last invitation to the marriage supper of the Lamb. Thousands of places that have not heard the call are yet to hear it. Many who have not given the message are yet to proclaim it. Again I appeal to our young men: Has not God called upon you to sound this message?—6T 412.

TALK, PRAY, BELIEVE.—The Lord is soon coming. Talk it, pray it, believe it. Make it a part of the life. You will have to meet a doubting, objecting spirit, but this will give way before firm, consistent trust in God. When perplexities or hindrances present themselves, lift the soul to God in songs of thanksgiving. Gird on the Christian armor, and be sure that your feet are "shod with the preparation of the gospel of peace." Preach the truth with boldness and fervor. Remember that the Lord looks in compassion upon this field and that He knows its poverty and its need. The efforts you are making will not prove a failure.—7T 237.

FILLED WITH JOY.—We should be filled with joy at the thought of Christ's soon appearing. To those that love His appearing He will come without sin unto salvation. But if our minds are filled with thoughts of earthly things, we cannot look forward with joy to His appearing.—Ms 11, 1885 quoted in HP 355.

WAIT CHEERFULLY.—The Lord is soon to come, and we must be prepared to meet Him in peace. Let us be determined to do all in our power to impart light to those around us. We are not to be sad, but cheerful, and we are to keep the Lord Jesus ever before us. . . . We must be ready and waiting for His appearing. Oh, how glorious it will be to see Him, and be welcomed as His redeemed ones! Long have we waited, but our faith is not to become weak. If we can but see the King in His beauty, we shall be forever and forever blessed. I feel as if I must cry aloud, "Homeward bound." We are nearing the time when Christ will come with power and great glory, to take His ransomed ones to their eternal home.—RH July 14, 1903 quoted in Mar 106.

Do Not Speculate About When the End Will Come.—The times and the seasons God has put in His own power. And why has not God given us this knowledge? Because we would not make a right use of it if He did. A condition of things would result from this knowledge among our people that would greatly retard the work of God in preparing a people to stand in the great day that is to come. We are not to live upon time excitement. We are not to be engrossed with speculations in regard to the times and the seasons which God has not revealed. Jesus has told His disciples to "watch," but not for a definite time. His followers are to be in the position of those who are listening for the orders of their Captain; they are to watch, wait, pray, and work, as they approach the time for the coming of the Lord; but no one will be able to predict just when that time will come; for "of that day and hour knoweth no man." You will not be able to say that He will come in one, two, or five years, neither are you to put off His coming by stating that it may not be for ten or twenty years.—RH March 22, 1892 quoted in 1SM 189.

CHAPTER

18

Heaven Can
Begin Now

HEAVEN IN HEART AND HOME.—[Our Saviour] wants us to trust in Him, believing His words so fully that we shall bring heaven into our lives here below. We can make heaven in heart and home as we pass along if our lives are hid with Christ in God. Thus we can bring joy and comfort into the lives of others. Christ's joy will remain in us, and our joy will be full.—Ms 28, 1901 quoted in 2SAT 147.

KINGDOM OF GRACE BEING ESTABLISHED.—The kingdom of God's grace is now being established, as day by day hearts that have been full of sin and rebellion yield to the sovereignty of His love. But the full establishment of the kingdom of His glory will not take place until the second coming of Christ to this world. "The kingdom and dominion, and the greatness of the kingdom under the whole

heaven," is to be given to "the people of the saints of the
Most High." Daniel 7:27. They shall inherit the kingdom
prepared for them "from the foundation of the world."
Matthew 25:34. And Christ will take to Himself His great
power and will reign.—MB 108.

HEAVEN IN THEIR HEARTS.—To His faithful followers
Christ has been a daily companion and familiar friend. They
have lived in close contact, in constant communion with
God. Upon them the glory of the Lord has risen. In them
the light of the knowledge of the glory of God in the face of
Jesus Christ has been reflected. Now they rejoice in the undimmed rays of the brightness and glory of the King in His
majesty. They are prepared for the communion of heaven;
for they have heaven in their hearts.—COL 421.

THE SWEETEST TYPE OF HEAVEN.—Home should be
made all that the word implies. It should be a little heaven
upon earth, a place where the affections are cultivated instead of being studiously repressed. Our happiness depends
upon this cultivation of love, sympathy, and true courtesy
to one another.—3T 539.

The sweetest type of heaven is a home where the Spirit
of the Lord presides. If the will of God is fulfilled, the husband and wife will respect each other and cultivate love
and confidence.—ST June 20, 1911 quoted in AH 15.

A PLEASANT AND CHEERFUL HOME CAN BE HEAVEN
ON EARTH.—Parents, make your home a little heaven

on earth. You can do this, if you so choose. You can make home so pleasant and cheerful that it will be the most attractive place on earth to your children. Let them receive all the blessings of the household. You can so relate yourselves to God that His Spirit will abide in your home. Come close to the bleeding side of the Man of Calvary. Those who are partakers with Him in His sufferings will at last be partakers with Him in His glory.—Ms 77, 1902 quoted in PCP 31.

OUR INSTITUTIONS CAN BE HEAVEN ON EARTH.—As sons and daughters of God, and members of the royal family, we are to learn of Him daily, that we may do His will and represent His character. The love of God received into the heart is an active power for good. It quickens the faculties of the mind and the powers of the soul; it enlarges the capacity for feeling, for loving. He who loves God supremely will love all the children of God. He will ever approach them with a respectful demeanor. And whatever his position of trust, his own considerate courtesy will win for him confidence and respect.

If this spirit pervaded our institutions, leading everyone to manifest toward his fellow-workers a love that is without dissimulation, these institutions would be a representation of heaven on earth. They would be a perpetual testimony to the world of what sanctifying truth can do when practiced by the receiver. Every man desires that this love may be exercised toward himself; and God calls upon him to reveal the same spirit toward others.—Ms 18, 1896 quoted in *1888,* 1356, 1357.

HEAVEN BEGINS HERE.—As through Jesus we enter into rest, heaven begins here. We respond to His invitation, Come, learn of Me, and in thus coming we begin the life eternal. Heaven is a ceaseless approaching to God through Christ. The longer we are in the heaven of bliss, the more and still more of glory will be opened to us; and the more we know of God, the more intense will be our happiness. As we walk with Jesus in this life, we may be filled with His love, satisfied with His presence. All that human nature can bear, we may receive here.—DA 331, 332.

When the Lord's people are filled with meekness and tenderness, they will realize that His banner over them is love, and His fruit will be sweet to their taste. They will make a heaven below in which to prepare for heaven above.—7T 131.

Heaven is to begin on this earth. . . .

He who receives Christ by living faith has a living connection with God. . . . He carries with him the atmosphere of heaven, which is the grace of God, a treasure that the world cannot buy.

If you would be a saint in heaven, you must first be a saint on earth.—Letter 18b, 1891 quoted in SD 112.

"His servants shall serve Him." Revelation 22:3. The life on earth is the beginning of the life in heaven; education on earth is an initiation into the principles of heaven; the lifework here is a training for the lifework there. What we now are, in character and holy service, is the sure foreshadowing of what we shall be.

"The Son of man came not to be ministered unto, but to minister." Matthew 20:28. Christ's work below is His work above, and our reward for working with Him in this world will be the greater power and wider privilege of working with Him in the world to come.

"Ye are My witnesses, saith the Lord, that I am God." Isaiah 43:12. This also we shall be in eternity.—Ed 307, 308.

The happiness of heaven will be found by conforming to the will of God, and if men become members of the royal family in heaven, it will be because heaven has begun with them on earth. . . . The righteous will take every grace, every precious, sanctified ability, into the courts above, and exchange earth for heaven. God knows who are the loyal and true subjects of His kingdom on earth, and those who do His will upon earth as it is done in heaven, will be made the members of the royal family above.—SD 361.

HEAVEN BEGINS IN THE SOUL.—Heaven begins in the soul, and as heavenly-mindedness increases, Christ is more and more appreciated, and finally becomes the Chiefest among ten thousand, the One altogether lovely. . . .

If we would see heaven, we must have heaven below. We must have a heaven to go to heaven in. We must have heaven in our families, through Christ continually approaching unto God. Christ is the great center of attraction, and the child of God hid in Christ, meets with God, and is lost in the divine being. Prayer is the life of the soul; it is feeding on Christ; it is turning our faces fully toward the Sun of Righteousness. As we turn our faces toward Him, He turns His face toward us. He longs to give us divine grace; and as we draw nigh to God with full assurance of faith, our spiritual conceptions are quickened. We do not then walk in blindness, bemoaning our spiritual barrenness; for by diligent, prayerful searching of the Word of God, we apply His rich promises unto our souls. Angels draw close to our side, and the enemy with his manifold devices is driven back.—ST July 31, 1893.

As our Redeemer leads us to the threshold of the Infinite, flushed with the glory of God, we may catch the themes of praise and thanksgiving from the heavenly choir round about the throne; and as the echo of the angels' song is awakened in our earthly homes, hearts will be drawn closer to the heavenly singers. Heaven's communion begins on earth. We learn here the keynote of its praise.—Ed 168.

LIFE-GIVING FRUIT OURS THROUGH CHRIST.—The fruit of the tree of life in the Garden of Eden possessed supernatural virtue. To eat of it was to live forever. Its fruit was the antidote of death. Its leaves were for the sustaining of life and immortality. But through man's disobedience, death entered the world. Adam ate of the tree of the knowledge of good and evil, the fruit of which he had been forbidden to touch. His transgression opened the floodgates of woe upon our race.

After the entrance of sin, the heavenly Husbandman transplanted the tree of life to the Paradise above; but its branches hang over the wall to the lower world. Through the redemption purchased by the blood of Christ, we may still eat of its life-giving fruit.

Of Christ it is written, "In him was life; and the life was the light of men." He is the fountain of life. Obedience to Him is the life-giving power that gladdens the soul.

Christ declares: "I am the bread of life; he that cometh to me shall never hunger; and he that believeth on me shall never thirst" [John 6:57, 63; Revelation 2:7, last part, quoted].—ST March 31, 1909 quoted in 7BC 988, 989.

BIBLE STUDY BRINGS HEAVEN TO CHURCH.—Christ and His Word are in perfect harmony. Received and obeyed, they open a sure path for the feet of all who are willing to walk in the light as Christ is in the light. If the people of God would appreciate His Word, we should have a heaven in the church here below. Christians would be eager, hungry, to search the Word. They would be anxious for time to compare scripture with scripture and to meditate upon the Word. They would be more eager for the light of the Word than for the morning paper, magazines, or novels. Their greatest desire would be to eat the flesh and drink the blood of the Son of God. And as a result their lives would be conformed to the principles and promises of the Word. Its instruction would be to them as the leaves of the tree of life. It would be in them a well of water, springing up into everlasting life. Refreshing showers of grace would refresh and revive the soul, causing them to forget all toil and weariness. They would be strengthened and encouraged by the words of inspiration.

Ministers would be inspired with divine faith. Their prayers would be characterized by earnestness, filled with the divine assurance of truth. Weariness would be forgotten in the sunlight of heaven. Truth would be interwoven with their lives, and its heavenly principles would be as a fresh, running stream, constantly satisfying the soul.—8T 193.

BY FAITH WE MAY STAND ON THE THRESHOLD.—What sustained the Son of God during His life of toil and sacrifice? He saw the results of the travail of His soul and was satisfied. Looking into eternity, He beheld the happiness of those who through His humiliation had received pardon and everlasting life. His ear caught the shout of the redeemed. He heard the ransomed ones singing the song of Moses and the Lamb.

We may have a vision of the future, the blessedness of heaven. In the Bible are revealed visions of the future glory, scenes pictured by the hand of God, and these are dear to His church. By faith we may stand on the threshold of the eternal city, and hear the gracious welcome given to those who in this life cooperate with Christ, regarding it as an honor to suffer for His sake.—AA 601.

God is not pleased to have His people hanging dark and painful pictures in memory's hall. He would have every soul plucking the roses and the lilies and the pinks, hanging memory's hall with the precious promises of God blooming all over the garden of God. He would have us dwelling upon them, our senses sharp and clear, taking them in their full richness, talking of the joy that is set before us. He would have us living in the world, yet not of it, our affections taking hold of eternal things. He would have us talking of the things which He has prepared for those that love Him. This will attract our minds, awaken our hopes and expectations, and strengthen our souls to endure the conflicts and trials of this life. As we dwell on these scenes the Lord will encourage our faith and confidence. He will draw aside the veil and give us glimpses of the saints' inheritance.—Ms 24, 1888 quoted in 3SM 163, 164.

Christ became one flesh with us, in order that we might become one spirit with Him. It is by virtue of this union that we are to come forth from the grave—not merely as a manifestation of the power of Christ, but because, through faith, His life has become ours. Those who see Christ in His true character, and receive Him into the heart, have everlasting life. It is through the Spirit that Christ dwells in us; and the Spirit of God, received into the heart by faith, is the beginning of the life eternal.—DA 388.

A Foretaste for the Humble.—We need Jesus abiding in the heart, a constant living wellspring; then the streams flowing from the living fountain will be pure, sweet, and heavenly. Then the foretaste of heaven will be given to the humble in heart.—Letter 37, 1887 quoted in CW 81.

Christ in the Soul Is Heaven.—Rest yourself wholly in the hands of Jesus. Contemplate His great love, and while you meditate upon His self-denial, His infinite sacrifice made in our behalf in order that we should believe in Him, your heart will be filled with holy joy, calm peace, and indescribable love. As we talk of Jesus, as we call upon Him in prayer, our confidence that He is our personal, loving Saviour will strengthen, and His character will appear more and more lovely. . . . We may enjoy rich feasts of love, and as we fully believe that we are His by adoption, we may have a foretaste of heaven.

Wait upon the Lord in faith. The Lord draws out the soul in prayer, and gives us to feel His precious love. We have a nearness to Him, and can hold sweet communion with Him. We obtain distinct views of His tenderness and compassion, and our hearts are broken and melted with contemplation of the love that is given to us. We feel indeed an abiding Christ in the soul. . . . Our peace is like a river, wave after wave of glory rolls into the heart, and indeed we sup with Jesus and He with us. We have a realizing sense of the love of God, and we rest in His love. No language can describe it, it is beyond knowledge. We are one with Christ, our life is hid with Christ in God. We have the assurance that when He who is our life shall appear, then shall we also appear with Him in glory. With strong confidence, we can call God our Father. Whether we live or die, we are the Lord's. His Spirit makes us like Jesus Christ in temper, and disposition, and we represent Christ to others.

When Christ is abiding in the soul the fact cannot be hid; for He is like a well of water springing up into everlasting life. We can but represent the likeness of Christ in our character, and our words, our deportment, produces in others a deep, abiding, increasing love for Jesus, and we make manifest . . . that we are conformed to the image of Jesus Christ.—Letter 52, 1894 quoted in SD 311.

CHAPTER

19

The Music of Heaven

A New Song About to Be Sung.—There is a day just about to burst upon us when God's mysteries will be seen, and all His ways vindicated; when justice, mercy, and love will be the attributes of His throne. When the earthly warfare is accomplished, and the saints are all gathered home, our first theme will be the song of Moses, the servant of God. The second theme will be the song of the Lamb, the song of grace and redemption. This song will be louder, loftier, and in sublimer strains, echoing and re-echoing through the heavenly courts. Thus the song of God's providence is sung, connecting the varying dispensations; for all is now seen without a veil between the legal, the prophetical, and the gospel.

The church history upon the earth and the church redeemed in heaven all center around the cross of Calvary. This is the theme, this is the song—Christ all and in all—in anthems of praise resounding through heaven from thousands and ten thousand times ten thousand and an innumerable company of the redeemed host. All unite in this song of Moses and of the Lamb. It is a new song, for it was never before sung in heaven.—TM 433.

ANGELS WELCOME THE KING AND HIS REDEEMED WITH A SONG OF TRIUMPH.—In that day the redeemed will shine forth in the glory of the Father and the Son. The angels, touching their golden harps, will welcome the King and His trophies of victory—those who have been washed and made white in the blood of the Lamb. A song of triumph will peal forth, filling all heaven. Christ has conquered. He enters the heavenly courts, accompanied by His redeemed ones, the witnesses that His mission of suffering and sacrifice has not been in vain.—9T 285, 286.

HEAVENLY MUSIC.—The prophet caught the sound of music there [in heaven], and song, such music and song as, save in the visions of God, no mortal ear has heard or mind conceived. "The ransomed of the Lord shall return, and come to Zion with songs and everlasting joy upon their heads: they shall obtain joy and gladness, and sorrow and sighing shall flee away." "Joy and gladness shall be found therein, thanksgiving, and the voice of melody." "As well the singers as the players on instruments shall be there." "They shall lift up their voice, they shall sing for the majesty of the Lord." Isaiah 35:10; 51:3; Psalm 87:7; Isaiah 24:14.—PK 730.

What a song that will be when the ransomed of the Lord meet at the gate of the Holy City, which is thrown back on its glittering hinges and the nations that have kept His word—His commandments—enter into the city, the crown of the overcomer is placed upon their heads, and the golden harps are placed in their hands! All heaven is filled with rich music, and with songs of praise to the Lamb. Saved, everlastingly saved, in the kingdom of glory! To have a life that measures with the life of God—that is the reward.—Ms 92, 1908 quoted in 7BC 982.

THE 144,000 SING THE SONG OF THEIR EXPERIENCE.—Upon the crystal sea before the throne, that sea of glass as it were mingled with fire—so resplendent is it with the glory of God—are gathered the company that have "gotten the victory over the beast, and over his image, and over his mark, and over the number of his name." With the Lamb upon Mount Zion, "having the harps of God," they stand, the hundred and forty and four thousand that were redeemed from among men; and there is heard, as the sound of many waters, and as the sound of a great thunder, "the voice of harpers harping with their harps." And they sing "a new song" before the throne, a song which no man can learn save the hundred and forty and four thousand. It is the song of Moses and the Lamb—a song of deliverance. None but the hundred and forty-four thousand can learn that song; for it is the song of their experience—an experience such as no other company have ever had. "These are they which follow the Lamb whithersoever He goeth." These, having been translated from the earth, from among the living, are counted as "the first fruits unto God and to the Lamb." Revelation 15:2, 3; 14:1-5.—GC 648, 649.

"In His temple doth everyone speak of His glory" (Psalm 29:9), and the song which the ransomed ones will sing—the song of their experience—will declare the glory of God: "Great and marvelous are Thy works, O Lord God, the Almighty; righteous and true are Thy ways, Thou King of the ages. Who shall not fear, O Lord, and glorify Thy name? For Thou only art holy." Revelation 15:3, 4, R.V.—Ed 308, 309.

The days of pain and weeping are forever ended. The King of glory has wiped the tears from all faces; every cause of grief has been removed. Amid the waving of palm branches they [the redeemed] pour forth a song of praise, clear, sweet, and harmonious; every voice takes up the strain, until the anthem swells through the vaults of heaven.—GC 650.

As the nations of the saved look upon their Redeemer and behold the eternal glory of the Father shining in His countenance; as they behold His throne which is from everlasting to everlasting, and know that His kingdom is to have no end, they break forth in rapturous song: "Worthy, worthy is the Lamb that was slain, and hath redeemed us to God by His own most precious blood!"—GC 651, 652.

THE REDEEMED WILL MAKE RICH MUSIC IN HEAVEN .—Then I saw a very great number of angels bring from the city glorious crowns—a crown for every saint, with his name written thereon. As Jesus called for the crowns, angels presented them to Him, and with His own right hand, the lovely Jesus placed the crowns on the heads of the saints. In the same manner the angels brought the harps, and Jesus presented them also to the saints. The commanding angels first struck the note, and then every voice was raised in grateful, happy praise, and every hand skillfully swept over the strings of the harp, sending forth melodious music in rich and perfect strains. Then I saw Jesus lead the redeemed company to the gate of the city. He laid hold of the gate and swung it back on its glittering hinges and bade the nations that had kept the truth enter in. Within the city there was everything to feast the eye. Rich glory they beheld everywhere. Then Jesus looked upon His redeemed saints; their countenances were radiant with glory; and as He fixed His loving eyes upon them, He said, with His rich, musical voice, "I behold the travail of My soul, and am satisfied. This rich glory is yours to enjoy eternally. Your sorrows are ended. There shall be no more death, neither sorrow nor crying, neither shall there be any more pain." I saw the redeemed host bow and cast their glittering crowns at the feet of Jesus, and then, as His lovely hand raised them up, they touched their golden harps and filled all heaven with their rich music and songs to the Lamb.—EW 288, 289.

Before entering the City of God, the Saviour bestows upon His followers the emblems of victory and invests them with the insignia of their royal state. The glittering ranks are drawn up in the form of a hollow square about their King, whose form rises in majesty high above saint and angel, whose countenance beams upon them full of benignant love. Throughout the unnumbered host of the redeemed every glance is fixed upon Him, every eye beholds

His glory whose "visage was so marred more than any man, and His form more than the sons of men." Upon the heads of the overcomers, Jesus with His own right hand places the crown of glory. For each there is a crown, bearing his own "new name" (Revelation 2:17), and the inscription, "Holiness to the Lord." In every hand are placed the victor's palm and the shining harp. Then, as the commanding angels strike the note, every hand sweeps the harp strings with skillful touch, awaking sweet music in rich, melodious strains. Rapture unutterable thrills every heart, and each voice is raised in grateful praise: "Unto Him that loved us, and washed us from our sins in His own blood, and hath made us kings and priests unto God and His Father; to Him be glory and dominion for ever and ever." Revelation 1:5, 6.—GC 645, 646.

THE PERFECT MUSIC OF HEAVEN.—I have been shown the order, the perfect order, of heaven, and have been enraptured as I listened to the perfect music there. After coming out of vision, the singing here has sounded very harsh and discordant. I have seen companies of angels, who stood in a hollow square, everyone having a harp of gold. At the end of the harp was an instrument to turn to set the harp or change the tunes. Their fingers did not sweep over the strings carelessly, but they touched different strings to produce different sounds. There is one angel who always leads, who first touches the harp and strikes the note, then all join in the rich, perfect music of heaven. It cannot be described. It is melody, heavenly, divine, while from every countenance beams the image of Jesus, shining with glory unspeakable.—1T 146.

A Song First Sung on Earth.—The redeemed cast their glittering crowns at the feet of Jesus; and then the angelic choir strikes the note of victory, and the angels in the two columns take up the song, and the redeemed host join as though they had been singing the song on the earth, and they have been.

Oh, what music! There is not an inharmonious note. Every voice proclaims, "Worthy is the Lamb that was slain." He sees of the travail of His soul, and is satisfied. Do you think anyone there will take time to tell of his trials and terrible difficulties? "The former shall not be remembered, nor come into mind." "God shall wipe away all tears from their eyes."—Ms 18, 1894 quoted in 6BC 1093.

Sing Heaven's Song Here.—Jesus is soon coming, and our position should be that of waiting and watching for His appearing. We should not allow anything to come in between us and Jesus. We must learn here to sing the song of heaven, so that when our warfare is over we can join in the song of the heavenly angels in the city of God. What is that song? It is praise, and honor, and glory unto Him that sitteth upon the throne, and unto the Lamb for ever and ever.—*Historical Sketches,* p. 145 quoted in LHU 372.

Every act, every deed of justice and mercy and benevolence, makes music in heaven.—RH August 16, 1881 quoted in ChS 100, 101.

As you open your door to Christ's needy and suffering ones, you are welcoming unseen angels. You invite the companionship of heavenly beings. They bring a sacred atmosphere of joy and peace. They come with praises upon their lips, and an answering strain is heard in heaven. Every deed of mercy makes music there. The Father from His throne numbers the unselfish workers among his most precious treasures.—DA 639.

20

A Call for Us
to Be There

BY FAITH BEHOLD ETERNITY.—The prophet caught the sound of music there [in the City of God], and song, such music and song as, save in the visions of God, no mortal ear has heard or mind conceived. "The ransomed of the Lord shall return, and come to Zion with songs and everlasting joy upon their heads: they shall obtain joy and gladness, and sorrow and sighing shall flee away." "Joy and gladness shall be found therein, thanksgiving, and the voice of melody." "As well the singers as the players on instruments shall be there." "They shall lift up their voice, they shall sing for the majesty of the Lord." Isaiah 35:10; 51:3; Psalm 87:7; Isaiah 24:14.

In the earth made new, the redeemed will engage in the occupations and pleasures that brought happiness to Adam and Eve in the beginning. The Eden life will be lived, the life in garden and field. "They shall build houses, and inhabit them; and they shall plant vineyards, and eat the fruit of them. They shall not build, and another inhabit; they shall not plant, and another eat: for as the days of a tree are the days of My people, and Mine elect shall long enjoy the work of their hands." Isaiah 65:21, 22.

There every power will be developed, every capability increased. The grandest enterprises will be carried forward, the loftiest aspirations will be reached, the highest ambitions realized. And still there will appear new heights to surmount, new wonders to admire, new truths to comprehend, fresh objects of study to call forth the powers of body and mind and soul.

The prophets to whom these great scenes were revealed longed to understand their full import. They "inquired and searched diligently: . . . searching what, or what manner of time the Spirit of Christ which was in them did signify. . . . Unto whom it was revealed, that not unto themselves, but unto us they did minister the things, which are now reported unto you." 1 Peter 1:10-12.

To us who are standing on the very verge of their fulfillment, of what deep moment, what living interest, are these delineations of the things to come—events for which, since our first parents turned their steps from Eden, God's children have watched and waited, longed and prayed!

Fellow pilgrim, we are still amid the shadows and turmoil of earthly activities; but soon our Saviour is to appear to bring deliverance and rest. Let us by faith behold the blessed hereafter as pictured by the hand of God. He who died for the sins of the world is opening wide the gates of Paradise to all who believe on Him. Soon the battle will have been fought, the victory won. Soon we shall see Him in whom our hopes of eternal life are centered. And in His presence the trials and sufferings of this life will seem as nothingness. The former things "shall not be remembered, nor come into mind."

"Cast not away therefore your confidence, which hath great recompense of reward. For ye have need of patience, that, after ye have done the will of God, ye might receive the promise. For yet a little while, and He that shall come will come, and will not tarry." "Israel shall be saved . . . with an everlasting salvation: ye shall not be ashamed nor confounded world without end." Isaiah 65:17; Hebrews 10:35-37; Isaiah 45:17.

Look up, look up, and let your faith continually increase. Let this faith guide you along the narrow path that leads through the gates of the city into the great beyond, the wide, unbounded future of glory that is for the redeemed. "Be patient therefore, brethren, unto the coming of the Lord. Behold, the husbandman waiteth for the precious fruit of the earth, and hath long patience for it, until he receive the early and latter rain. Be ye also patient; stablish your hearts: for the coming of the Lord draweth nigh." James 5:7, 8.

The nations of the saved will know no other law than the law of heaven. All will be a happy, united family, clothed with the garments of praise and thanksgiving. Over the scene the morning stars will sing together, and the sons of God will shout for joy, while God and Christ will unite in proclaiming. "There shall be no more sin, neither shall there be any more death."

"And it shall come to pass, that from one new moon to another, and from one Sabbath to another, shall all flesh come to worship before Me, saith the Lord." "The glory of the Lord shall be revealed, and all flesh shall see it together." "The Lord God will cause righteousness and praise to spring forth before all the nations." "In that day shall the Lord of hosts be for a crown of glory, and for a diadem of beauty, unto the residue of His people."

"The Lord shall comfort Zion: He will comfort all her waste places; and He will make her wilderness like Eden, and her desert like the garden of the Lord." "The glory of Lebanon shall be given unto it, the excellency of Carmel and Sharon." "Thou shalt no more be termed Forsaken; neither shall thy land any more be termed Desolate: but thou shalt be called My Delight, and thy land Beulah. . . . As the bridegroom rejoiceth over the bride, so shall thy God rejoice over thee." Isaiah 66:23; 40:5; 61:11; 28:5; 51:3; 35:2; 62:4, 5, margin.—PK 730-733.

ON THE VERGE OF FULFILLMENT.—We are living in a most solemn period of this earth's history. There is never time to sin; it is always perilous to continue in transgression, but in a special sense is this true at the present time. We are now upon the very borders of the eternal world and stand in a more solemn relation to time and to eternity than ever before. Now let every person search his own heart and plead for the bright beams of the Sun of

Righteousness to expel all spiritual darkness and cleanse from defilement.

To us who are standing on the very verge of their fulfillment, of what deep moment, what living interest, are these delineations of the things to come—events for which, since our first parents turned their steps from Eden, God's children have watched and waited, longed and prayed!

Fellow pilgrim, we are still amid the shadows and turmoil of earthly activities, but soon our Saviour is to appear to bring deliverance and rest. Let us by faith behold the blessed hereafter, as pictured by the hand of God.—AH 549, 550.

An Appeal for Personal Preparation.—I urge you to prepare for the coming of Christ in the clouds of heaven. Day by day cast the love of the world out of your hearts. Understand by experience what it means to have fellowship with Christ. Prepare for the judgment, that when Christ shall come to be admired in all them that believe, you may be among those who will meet Him in peace.— 9T 285.

We Are Homeward Bound.—We are still amidst the shadows and turmoil of earthly activities. Let us consider most earnestly the blessed hereafter. Let our faith pierce through every cloud of darkness and behold Him who died for the sins of the world. He has opened the gates of paradise to all who receive and believe on Him. To them He gives power to become the sons and daughters of God. Let the afflictions which pain us so grievously become instructive lessons, teaching us to press forward toward the mark of the prize of our high calling in Christ. Let us be encouraged by the thought that the Lord is soon to come. Let this hope gladden our hearts. "Yet a little while, and He that shall come will come, and will not tarry." Hebrews 10:37. Blessed are those servants who, when their Lord comes, shall be found watching.

We are homeward bound. He who loved us so much as to die for us hath builded for us a city. The New Jerusalem is our place of rest. There will be no sadness in the city of God. No wail of sorrow, no dirge of crushed hopes and buried affections, will evermore be heard. Soon the garments of heaviness will be changed for the wedding garment. Soon we shall witness the coronation of our King. Those whose lives have been hidden with Christ, those who on this earth have fought the good fight of faith, will shine forth with the Redeemer's glory in the kingdom of God.

It will not be long till we shall see Him in whom our hopes of eternal life are centered. And in His presence, all the trials and sufferings of this life will be as nothingness. "Cast not away therefore your confidence, which hath great recompense of reward. For ye have need of patience, that, after ye have done the will of God, ye might receive the promise. For yet a little while, and He that shall come will come, and will not tarry." Verses 35-37. Look up, look up, and let your faith continually increase. Let this faith guide you along the narrow path that leads through the gates of the city of God into the great beyond, the wide, unbounded

future of glory that is for the redeemed. "Be patient therefore, brethren, unto the coming of the Lord. Behold, the
husbandman waiteth for the precious fruit of the earth,
and hath long patience for it, until he receive the early and
latter rain. Be ye also patient; stablish your hearts: for the
coming of the Lord draweth nigh." James 5:7, 8.—9T 286-
288.

THE GREAT CONTROVERSY IS ENDED; SIN IS NO
MORE.—And the years of eternity, as they roll, will bring
richer and still more glorious revelations of God and of
Christ. As knowledge is progressive, so will love, reverence, and happiness increase. The more men learn of
God, the greater will be their admiration of His character. As Jesus opens before them the riches of redemption and the amazing achievements in the great controversy with Satan, the hearts of the ransomed thrill with
more fervent devotion, and with more rapturous joy they
sweep the harps of gold; and ten thousand times ten
thousand and thousands of thousands of voices unite to
swell the mighty chorus of praise.

"And every creature which is in heaven, and on the
earth, and under the earth, and such as are in the sea, and
all that are in them, heard I saying, Blessing, and honor,
and glory, and power, be unto Him that sitteth upon the
throne, and unto the Lamb for ever and ever." Revelation
5:13.

The great controversy is ended. Sin and sinners are no
more. The entire universe is clean. One pulse of harmony and
gladness beats through the vast creation. From Him who cre-

ated all, flow life and light and gladness, throughout the realms of illimitable space. From the minutest atom to the greatest world, all things, animate and inanimate, in their unshadowed beauty and perfect joy, declare that God is love.—GC 678.